The Long Way Home

The Long Way Home

The Powerful 4-Step Plan for Adult Children of Divorce

M. GARY NEUMAN, LMHC

WILEY

Cover Design: Wendy Mount

Published by John Wiley & Sons, Inc., Hoboken, New Jersey
Published simultaneously in Canada

Text design by Forty-five Degree Design LLC

For general information about our other products and services, please contact our Customer Care Department within the United States at (800) 762-2974, outside the United States at (317) 572-3993 or fax (317) 572-4002.

Wiley also publishes its books in a variety of electronic formats and by print-on-demand. Some content that appears in standard print versions of this book may not be available in other formats. For more information about Wiley products, visit us at www.wiley.com.

Library of Congress Cataloging-in-Publication Data:

Neuman, M. Gary.
The long way home : the powerful 4-step plan for adult children of divorce / M. Gary Neuman.
    p. cm.
  Includes index.
   ISBN 978-0-470-40922-0 (pbk.); ISBN 978-1-118-21923-2 (ebk);
   ISBN 978-0-470-45027-7 (ebk) — ISBN 978-1-118-21924-9 (ebk)
  1. Adult children of divorced parents.   2. Children of divorced parents.   I. Title.
HQ777.5.N483 2013
  306.89–dc23

                                                                2012031776

Printed in the United States of America

10 9 8 7 6 5 4 3 2 1

For Mom

Contents

PART 3
Resolving Major Issues

A Note to Readers

All stories in this book are true and are told in each individual's own words. Every person represented in this book has been part of Gary's research and has not seen Gary for any form of personal therapy. Names and identifying information have been changed in order to protect their anonymity.

Acknowledgments

To all of the participants in my research who then used this book and shared their very hearts and souls. Your struggles, hard work to change, and desire to share with others in the hope of helping them is so admirable. You represent the very best of what we are as people. I hope I've honored your disclosures with respect and that others can benefit and grow from your participation in this book.

Esther Neuman, MSW, for the incredible work and countless hours of work. Your help with the research, contact with participants, and organization have given beautiful voice to those who share their very depths in this book. You handled the interviews with such sensitivity and warmth. Your willingness to help is so appreciated. Mom and I are blessed to have you as our daughter.

Carol Mann, my amazing agent. Thanks for believing in this project. You're always there to answer every call and make this book better. Your professionalism is unmatched.

Debora Yost, for your outstanding editing assistance. Thanks for being there so many times and genuinely caring about the help this book offers.

My editor, Tom Miller, for your excellent suggestions. You always care deeply about my work and it shows with your energy and desire to help me create the best books in me. We did it again!

My copyeditor, Judith Antonelli, and production editor Hope Breeman, for making this book proper and keeping it on schedule.

And on a personal note: my wife, Melisa. After twenty-five years, I can't distinguish where I begin or end without you. We are one soul. Your overwhelming love, care, and warmth fuel my every moment. Thank you for your goodness and the passionate spirit you bring to our lives.

My children, Yehuda, Esther, Michael, Pacey, and Daniel. The love we have is my life. You have grown into adults and each of you makes us so proud. All of you are always there to learn together, laugh together, and listen together. I am blessed to have each of you in my life.

To everyone in the Neuman and Simons clan. I am supported by all of you and wouldn't be anywhere if it were not for each one of you. Thank you for the strength you give me every day.

Bonnie, for still being the smartest person I know and for your graciousness.

The One Above, who does not need anything from me and yet still wants to believe in me. Thanks for Your blessings. I hope I have made You proud and have properly reflected Your goodness.

What Readers Are Saying

Reading Gary Neuman's book and participating in his program have allowed me to see hope in my life. It sounds like a cliché to say it, but before participating in the program, a perpetual cloud cover followed me. Now, thanks to this book, the clouds are passing and I can feel the sun shining on my life.

Reading this book made me feel like I was receiving advice from a friend who knew exactly what I was going through. I couldn't believe that someone was able to relate to my experiences so clearly. Gary explained what I always knew—that my parents' divorce, even though I was very young, altered the direction my life would take, how I would view myself, and the relationships I would make.

As I worked the program, I had insights that stopped me in my tracks. At times some of the memories were so painful I wasn't sure I could go on with the program, but Gary's encouraging words helped me persevere. By the time I got to the part on change, I was so at ease with my journaling. Each day I could actually put on paper who I wanted to be and how I wanted to act. Amazingly, many days the exact things I wrote down came to be!

The snowball effect continues to this day. I have gained more self-confidence. I am a more positive thinker. I am aware of my limitations and love myself in spite of them. I have created boundaries. I do not tolerate people treating me badly. I love myself more than I ever have. And, in turn, possibly for the first time, I am loving others—truly. I am grateful for it all.

I am still a work in progress. I will read this book again and am glad that I have it as a resource whenever I need to brush up on my awareness. The tenets in Gary's plan are simple, but I am the proof they can lead you out of a dark place.

—Laura Tyson, an infant when her parents divorced

Before I heard about Gary Neuman's book, I was not a believer in self-help books. I looked and read through many, but they were always disappointing. They never hit a chord with me—an adult who had been a child of divorce. I wasn't happy, and I guess I knew I needed some direction, some help. Then I spotted Gary's book. Never in a million years would it have ever occurred to me that my parents' divorce could be the source of my discontent and lack of direction in life. What an eye-opening revelation!

Reading this book and following the program has been life altering. It has helped me understand why I did the things I did growing up and how I wound up making certain adult choices. All the things I had been keeping secret in my life were there in black and white on the page.

Obviously, I never wanted to repeat my parents' mistakes, but Gary made me see that their mistakes were all

I had to go on. It wasn't my fault! Taking the journey into my past to where I am now has been remarkable. It hasn't been fun, but I recognize that it was necessary. I have to say, change *is* good!

—Elizabeth O'Donnell, ten years old when her parents divorced

I have been through many arenas of healing—workshops, inner child work, therapy, seminars, countless self-help books and tapes—but this program has allowed me to really feel my hurt and find a place to start healing the wounds that have piggybacked with me since I was eleven years old. I finally have a handle on my life and my life's path. My relationships are clear to me. I am able to look at my old patterns of thinking and acting and see that now I am free to live outside the box of fear and self-doubt. Today I am truly looking at and living life from a safer place. I am on top of my own life. I can make choices that are right for me. Feeling love for myself and for everyone in my life has been one of the biggest results of this compassionate and thoughtful book. The outcome has been magical.

—Amy Maron, thirteen years old when her parents divorced

This program has meant the world to me. It has changed my life, and I keep this book by my bedside. I am eight months into the program and write in my journal every night.

I was one of those guys who said you should never go back and talk about your past. "Grow up," I'd tell my brothers whenever they'd begin to talk about Mom leaving us and Dad barely caring for our needs. But after being unable to maintain a relationship with a woman and then having two children with women I barely knew, I had to find help.

Gary Neuman's program is so clear, direct, and real. It allowed me to open up my past, learn from it, and grow into a much more aware person.

We can all learn how to "re-right" our childhood and not be a slave to it.

—Zachary J., seven years old when his parents divorced

Preface

The first time I witnessed the devastation of divorce was twenty-five years ago, when I was helping judges in the Miami-Dade, Florida, court system assess the home environment of parents seeking a divorce. My primary responsibility was to report back and recommend which parent would be the better primary caregiver for their children—what Florida at the time termed the *primary residential parent*. I was also to advise judges on how much access the nonresident parent should have to his or her children.

It was quite an awesome responsibility, which I took very seriously; however, I could see there was an obvious wrong taking place: I, a perfect stranger, after visiting and talking to everyone in each home for one or two hours, had a say about where these children of divorce were going to live until they were ready to make it on their own.

It was heart wrenching to witness the process in which two parents losing control over their lives through their failed marriage became even more powerless by entering a court that was going to dictate the basic living arrangements of their children. These families were out of control, and what they really needed was a way to get back in control. Instead, they'd squabble and fight over who was right and who was wrong and reach an impasse about what was really best for their kids. The court was placed in the absurd position of making the decision for them.

The idea that a court system with little knowledge of a family's life together had the power to make a decision that would affect children for the rest of their lives seemed ludicrous, sad, and even a bit scary. But in lieu of something better, it seemed appropriate at the time.

I was hands-on involved in the process. I was an eyewitness to the devastation of divorce in virtually every home I entered. I spoke to each family member privately and often met with each one twice. I listened as each parent spat on about the failings of the other. I'd spend time talking to the children and listening to them go on about their lives and reveal their dreams. I felt their fear and heartache over what was happening in their home, many of them much too young to comprehend what was unraveling before them.

The way these kids presented themselves was quite different from one household to the next, depending on their home environment. One child would be sharply oppositional, another quiet and shy, and yet another verbal and outraged over the family situation. Often, after meeting everyone, I felt like I was making my recommendations based on the lesser of two evils. Imagine—what a way to grow up! Many of these kids didn't stand a chance of having the normal, happy childhood that all kids deserve.

This is not to say that these parents did not love their children. They did, but the profoundly corrosive feelings that splintered their marriage overpowered any understanding of the effect that divorce was having on their kids and would continue to have afterward. They honestly felt that what they were doing was best for themselves and their children.

It is amazing to me how often parents just don't get it. I found it so ironic that parents would try to explain that they were getting divorced "for the sake of the children"—to put an end to the fighting, hostilities, and mistreatment. Yet they'd speak with such venom—or, in some cases, with utter powerlessness—that I instinctively knew life really wasn't going to change much for their children, no matter which household they'd end up in. The anger, fighting, and emotional abuse that they described to me, often in vivid detail, were sure to continue, perhaps with a different story line but with the same sad and painful outcome for the children.

Of course, this is not to say that all of the families I visited in those days were self-destructing. I also talked to parents who were calm and working well together through divorce; however, they were the exception and not the norm. But even in the "best" situations, the children still pay in some way. Divorce brings closure to a bad situation and a chance to start over and find happiness for Mom and Dad. But for their children, the wounds remain open. Shattered marriages shatter children. In the end it is the kids who are left staring at the pieces, totally bewildered about how the family can ever be whole again.

My work was quite an experience and paved the way for what was to come.

Introduction

Sandcastles for Adults

I t's a mistake when grown-ups think they understand the problems children experience going through their parents' divorce. Very seldom do the adults get it right. It's as though they think an imaginary stopwatch begins to tick a better life into existence the moment a judge signs the divorce decree. The judge may be signing away the years of turmoil for the parents, but it doesn't erase what the children have already endured. Nor does it ease the path they will have to follow going through life as a child of divorce.

Think about it for a moment. It takes a lot of negative emotion to push parents into divorce. The vast majority of parents endure many years of emotional pain but avoid the subject of divorce for the sake of their children. Yet endurance, especially when it feels like it's eroding your existence, can last only so long. Eventually, some incident pushes one parent (or sometimes both parents) into the corner of "I can't take it anymore." Divorce is often a powerless, desperate end-of-my-rope step taken without much thought and consideration for what is truly coming next. Typically, the marriage is so broken that no one knows what else to do but end it.

If you can imagine the behind-the-scenes picture of what produces these desperate feelings and leads to a couple's decision to split, you can see how the other victims in this scenario— the children—have already endured years of family trauma. They've heard the cruel comments, witnessed the fights, and watched their parents drift into leading separate lives long before the words *separation* and *divorce* ever entered their vocabulary. For many children, it's a family scene that has defined their entire lives. The divorce is but a demoralizing detour on a lifelong journey through family sadness.

When parents decide to divorce, it is as good as asking their children to choose the parent they love more, even though those words are never spoken. Nevertheless, the tug-of-war is on. Children feel like they're betraying one parent if they accept an invitation to do something with the other. They get roped into keeping secrets from a parent. Some are even forced to carry hostile messages back and forth between the parents. They can't help but feel the hostility of one for the other.

Parents are a lifeline to their children, and it is traumatic for kids to see the line unravel. Betrayal weighs heavily when they feel they must take sides. When they do, they fear the other parent will love them less. They fear one parent will get angry if they "tell" on the other. And then when one parent brings a new love interest into the frazzle, the children fear they may lose the parent completely—or worse, have to share him or her with other kids they don't even know.

Welcome to the world of children of divorce.

Working with troubled families, especially those in the throes of divorce, is hard on the psyche. Images of these children in their emotional turmoil get branded on the brain. It made me realize: if I can't get the pictures out of *my* mind, imagine what it's like for the children! I knew I needed to do more to stop the continuum of powerlessness for broken families. They needed guidance to gain back a sense of normalcy instead of just giving in to the idea that they were from one messed-up family. They needed to feel grounded as a family. So I decided to develop some innovative ways to help.

Whenever I talked to children of divorce, I found that they all felt quite different, but not in a good way. Mostly they felt alone and isolated, abandoned by their protectors. Even though there were plenty of other kids going through the same thing, they felt it was happening only to them. Divorce was a shameful secret they didn't want to get out. They didn't talk about it at school or with friends. It was just too painful and embarrassing. They kept their thoughts and emotions locked up inside. I thought, if they could only realize that they were hardly alone with their feelings, it would give them some comfort.

I was convinced that if I could get these kids together to interact with one another, they would see that they were not different. It would boost their confidence and self-esteem. They'd feel safer, and they would smile. They would shed the shame of feeling like peculiar children from strange, broken families. Rather, they'd see themselves as kids who have a common bond with many other kids their own age whose feelings are remarkably similar to their own.

I called the program Sandcastles, and it worked beautifully from the start. The first groups were nothing less than magical. The children were bursting to share their most heartfelt emotions, as though they'd been gagged for years. As group leader, I needed only to get them started. The rest was meaningful dialogue portrayed through artwork, poetry, and role-playing—all from their individual perspectives.

In order to give the parents a sense of what was taking place, I invited them to return for the end of the program. The children invited the parents to participate and share their feelings in a safe and emotion-building environment. It was a learning experience for everybody, including myself.

Miami-Dade, Florida, became the first county in the United States that would not grant a divorce in a family with children between the ages of six and seventeen until the children completed the Sandcastles program.

That was fifteen years ago. Since then, the Sandcastles program has been mandatory in counties in fourteen states and operates in districts of Canada, Mexico, England, and South Africa. More than three hundred thousand children of divorce have completed Sandcastles, and it continues to help children of divorce share their deepest emotions and gain a feeling of normalcy.

Nothing can heal the wounds of divorce, but Sandcastles became the much-needed medicine to reduce the symptoms.

My wife came up with the name Sandcastles because of its imagery: a child sculpting a castle on a wet and sandy shore. Everyone who's ever built a sandcastle near the ocean's edge knows that the tide will wear it down, yet that doesn't deter the child. The child will be determined to rebuild, fervently digging and shifting sand in order to repair the castle and make it even stronger than before.

It is that image of a child enthusiastically rebuilding a sandcastle that my wife and I wanted to offer children of divorce. All children are capable of helping themselves, and they shouldn't believe that the only solution is to wait for an adult to come to their rescue. Sitting back and letting adults manage everything didn't work much during the tumultuous years before the divorce, so why expect it now?

But since when do kids believe they can rebuild their emotional lives? Where do the tools come from? The Sandcastles program teaches children of divorce that they are wise and capable people, entitled to their feelings, and capable of finding ways to cope. I am thankful that I was blessed to play a role in seeing so many children benefit from Sandcastles, yet I couldn't help but wish that every child of divorce could have the opportunity to go through the Sandcastles experience. To this end I wrote *Helping Your Kids Cope with Divorce the Sandcastles Way* so parents everywhere could learn from its principles and apply them to their family's lives.

Sandcastles has helped a lot of children and continues to do so. Nevertheless, it has missed an opportunity to help a special segment of children of divorce: those who are now adults. That is why I wrote this book. There are millions of adults who experienced the trauma of going through their parents' divorce twenty, thirty, forty, or more years ago. Few have found closure; most have not. It is a time in a child's life that is never forgotten. It stays with you; it is part of who you are. There is not an adult who was a child of divorce who does not have vivid memories of what those days were like.

If you are holding this book in your hands, it is likely that you are still feeling the wounds of your parents' divorce. As you are about to find out, you are far from alone. My life has largely been dedicated to bettering the lives of children of divorce, and now I want to help the children who are grown up. Like Sandcastles, this book is designed to help you rebuild your past, regardless of how long you have believed you couldn't.

I call this adult program Re-Right Your Past, because you will spend five weeks reliving your past, but from a different vantage point. You can't change the past, but you can go back and understand it in a new, more objective way. So you will rewrite *and* "re-right," or make right again, your personal history. You will change your present and future by changing the way you see and understand your past.

Re-Right Your Past is quite different from Sandcastles, but the goals are the same. After all, you're not a kid anymore, and there is a lot more baggage to sort through and discard. You will feel lots of empathy going through the program, but there is no coddling. I will be taking you back to some dark places in your life—times long forgotten and some you wish you could forget but can't. It is a very necessary step in the four-step process that will lead you to much-needed change and get you to be who you want to be and point you in the direction you want to go.

The success of re-righting is dependent on two things: introspection and keeping a journal (there will be lots of both). Don't let this put you off. The first reaction from everyone who hears the task-driven nature of this program goes something like "I don't have that kind of time," or "That's not me," or "I am just not comfortable writing." This is why I am offering you plenty of help.

Before I wrote this book, I enlisted the help of hundreds of people to participate in a pilot research program. Throughout the book, I will share the thoughts and feelings from the private journals of these re-righting grads. Their names, of course, have been changed to protect their privacy. When you're staring at a blank page or are uncertain how to express yourself, you can turn to their stories and personal journal entries for help and inspiration. You're likely to see yourself in many of the stories.

These stories are from men and women from all walks of life who share one characteristic: they are all adults who were children of divorce. They learned through Re-Right Your Past that you are not defined by your past. You are not immune to having a true love and good, trusting relationships. It is even possible to heal the open wounds that still make life with one parent or both a struggle, no matter how much distance is between you.

This book is about connecting you with so many others who feel your pain and have found ways to come to terms with it. We can all take this journey together. I will lead the way, but in the end, you'll get to where you need to go while finding your own incredible strength.

Thank you for giving me the opportunity to be part of changing your life and your desire to heal from your past.

PART 1

Adults Who Were Children of Divorce

1

You Are Normal

As an adult who was a child of divorce, you are faced with a severe conflict that is unique: a mixed bag of feelings weighed down by the sense that nobody wants to hear about it. *Get over it,* your mind keeps repeating, even if your family and friends stopped saying it to you a long time ago. After all, lots of people went through what you did as a kid. Who wants to hear about it? *Move on, get yourself together, stop whining. How long can you keep rehashing the same old stuff? Give it up!*

It doesn't help when you don't have the ear of a compassionate friend who can listen to you. Or maybe you don't want to talk about it. You've *never* wanted to talk about it. Not talking about it and not having someone to talk to, however, only prevent you from accepting what is pent up deep down: the family dysfunction that filled your childhood is seeping into your adult life and wreaking a new kind of havoc.

You suppress as best you can the lingering emotional trauma you felt when your dad or your mom walked out of the house and splintered your family in two. The fear, desperation, and hurt may have faded, but they never go away completely. Feelings of insecurity can pop up at any time in your life: at work, when meeting new people, when making major life decisions, when tucking your kids into bed at night. You'd like to believe it's all behind you now, but you know it isn't, and you can't really talk about it. You keep your feelings and insecurities a secret, just as you did as a child. The truth is, you're not much different from every child who walks into a Sandcastles program: wounded, sad, and wondering if it's worse for you than it is for everybody else. The only difference is that you're now grown up.

You're probably troubled about what is wrong with you and why you are unable to get past your past the way everyone else from a broken family does. But I have news for you: everyone else doesn't. The fallout from divorce follows children into adulthood and can last for a lifetime.

Unfortunately, adults who were children of divorce don't always recognize this as the root of their issues in life. It is divorce's nasty little secret. It's why you are afraid of sounding weak if you talk about it—to others as well as to yourself. It's understandable. After all, you don't want to think that life is holding you back just because of what happened to you as a child, especially because it wasn't your fault. Unfortunately, pretending the feelings away won't get you to where you want to be.

This is why I have a favor to ask, which I promise you'll be glad you granted. As we embark on this program of renewal, I ask that you allow yourself to reopen the part of yourself that knows deep down how much your parents' divorce and its aftermath have affected you. My ability to help you heal and change depends on your willingness to remember the real you: the good, the not so good, and the regrets that are part of you. To do any less is to deny crucial facts about your life that are going to be important when you read about the similar experiences of others.

My Research

A lot of what I know about the long, lingering effects of divorce comes from men and women just like yourself whom I've met and counseled during my twenty-five years as a therapist specializing in family struggles. The childhood experience of living through parental divorce is a common thread in the problems that bring many adults to therapy. That reality and the Sandcastles program were the impetus for the Re-Right Your Past program and this book. But before I could write, I needed to find out just how deep and profound these struggles really are. So I set out to do research in the form of an online survey that asked adults who were children of divorce specific questions about how the family breakup affected them. In the end, responses from 379 men and women qualified for scientific scrutiny.

I know as well as any other therapist that the devastating effects of parental divorce follow children into adulthood, but the outpouring of emotion I found while reading the survey results was quite overwhelming. The survey proved one thing for certain: the issues you have as an adult are common and rooted in the turmoil of your parents' divorce. So I need you to stop hiding from the truth. Stop worrying about what other people say. If others can't empathize, then they either didn't experience divorce as a child or they are in denial.

The first step in helping yourself is to open up and allow yourself to recognize how your parents' divorce has affected you. However, I promise that you will not remain mired in the problems created by your past. You will not get stuck there. This book is designed to help you change your life, but nothing can change if you are hiding. So open up. Look in the mirror and see yourself as you are, with all of your emotional scars. Your willingness to be honest about your feelings, no matter how deeply hidden they are, is absolutely necessary for you to heal and reach closure.

If you've always thought no one else could really understand, you now know that you were wrong. I have 379 people with a resounding "I understand!" to help you move on and heal the wounds. Just look at how these newfound friends float your boat. The results of my research showed the following about adults who were children of divorce:

- The majority feel that their parents' divorce has under-mined their self-confidence and their ability to trust.
- 89 percent believe that their parents' divorce clearly had a negative effect on their lives, and 45 percent of those label the effect as severe.
- 80 percent experience severe sadness or depression.
- Marital issues are common. Only 37 percent are in a first marriage, which means that 63 percent have divorced, are widowed, or have never been married.
- 80 percent of those who are married fear that their own marriages may end in divorce.
- 72 percent believe that their parents' divorce affected their ability to sustain close relationships.
- 52 percent say they lack self-confidence in love relationships.
- 46 percent fear that their spouses are cheating on them.
- 46 percent feel unexplained guilt.
- 43 percent have difficulty dealing with conflict.
- 43 percent suffer from anxiety.
- 43 percent are distrustful of love.
- 37 percent have serious fears about money.
- 37 percent fear being taken advantage of by others.
- 33 percent have a temper problem.

Most interesting, people who expressed these negative outcomes said they were "seriously contributed to by my parents' divorce."

Imagine: 89 percent of adults who were children of divorce say that their parents' divorce has had a negative effect on their lives. That's a heady statistic. It's something important to keep in mind; it tells you that you are certainly not alone! You're one of millions trying to manage life while sweeping the thoughts of your past under the rug. It's your way of moving on, and it is quite understandable. You may not realize quite how much being a child of divorce has affected you. Most people don't.

How You Managed as a Child

The insidious nature of divorce puts children in an emotionally precarious position: on their own with their feelings. Most children don't like talking about the divorce, and they are even less likely to express how they feel about it. Think for a moment about your own feelings about your parents' divorce. They weren't pleasant feelings, were they?

Being left alone to manage your own feelings is a dangerous situation for a child of divorce. To survive emotionally, you desperately want to soften the intensity of your feelings, but you can do so only by cutting off part of those feelings, swallowing them, or hiding them. Managing your feelings in this manner has the potential to leave you numb. Kids caught up in an atmosphere of hostility tend to play mental games to soften the reality of what's occurring around them. When your parents were arguing, perhaps you buried your head in your pillow or talked to your dog about something unrelated in order to divert your attention from the fighting in the other room.

Kids of divorce can't even begin to deal with their feelings, at least not in a healthy way. They simply don't have the capacity to do so. They therefore have no choice but to find a way to manage them. Basically, they run from them in a desperate effort to stifle the hurt in order to get on with life. Sound familiar?

It's almost instinctive to respond in this way. Imagine what it would be like if, as a child, you allowed yourself to wallow in the intensity of every horrible moment. You'd be unable to function and would possibly become suicidal in time. A child's mind protects itself from unrelenting emotional pain by diverting its attention. Some kids delude themselves through imagination: "Mommy and Daddy are really happy." Or when their feelings overwhelm them, they release them through tears, anger, or acting out. For some kids, finding ways to manage their emotions becomes impossible. They completely shut down and become largely numb to all feelings.

Look Who's Talking—and Who's Not

Did you talk about your feelings? Chances are you didn't. My research found that an astonishing 53 percent of adults who were children of divorce have never spoken about their parents' divorce. My research also found the following:

- 70 percent were never taken to a therapist as a child.
- Only 16 percent who went to therapy as a child found it helpful.
- 49 percent found therapy helpful as an adult.
- 41 percent have never gone to therapy.

Hiding behind a Facade

Children of divorce face a life of surmounting difficulties, starting with a childhood that was taken away too fast. Let me explain what I mean.

Perhaps when you were a child, you looked okay to others—just an ordinary kid like any other. It's the image you wanted to project. It was your coping strategy to make everything seem okay, even to yourself. It was you on the outside, and you hoped that somehow it would magically make you okay on the inside. You didn't—actually, you *couldn't*—think it through, or you would have realized that this would not happen through osmosis.

You can't make your feelings go away just because you wish them away. You may have been able to wish them away with the facade you displayed, but that's all it was: a front for your true feelings, the real you. However, you let it be and made believe, because it was a shield from your emotional pain. You tried hard to never let it show, even though you felt the pain.

Looking back, you might now realize that the way you managed your emotions during this tumultuous time of life explains a lot of your behavior growing up, some of which you might regret. Perhaps you were anxious, angry, moody, shy, promiscuous, or a late bloomer or you did poorly in school—all a result of your incapacity to capture a feeling of self-worth. This too is understandable. After all, how is it possible to feel good about yourself when your home life, the very basis for your entire sense of self, has been torn apart, even called "broken" in society's terminology? How could you, the child of a broken home, feel much other than broken yourself?

You Don't Have to Hide from Yourself

Nobody wants to feel like a victim, but hiding from yourself is never a good option. So it's time to heal. No more hiding. Allow yourself to look back at your childhood and see how it has affected your life now. Be courageous enough to revisit your full-blown feelings and memories. Just knowing that you are like every other kid who was in a similar circumstance, the house of divorce, can help you to find the strength to begin to heal.

Most important, keep in mind that there's nothing wrong with you. Rather, there was something wrong with the circumstances that cornered you into a certain way of thinking and feeling in order for you to survive. No other kid in the same situation could have managed any better. Once you can allow yourself to feel normal, you can begin to find ways to change your life and heal from your past.

In the upcoming chapters, I'm going to ask you to make a leap toward healing. The process will bring up uncomfortable thoughts and memories, but this time you won't be trying to bury them. You will be able to learn from them and change your life.

2

You Can Re-Right
Your Past

When we think of emotional healing, we tend to conjure up images of mountaintops, deep breathing, and forgiveness. But passivity never healed anyone. You can't just sit there and wish your past away. It simply won't work. However, it is an instinct many troubled people choose to follow.

I understand why we like to be passive. Usually it's because we just don't know what to do about our troubles in life. If I were locked in a dark room and bumped into something threatening, and I had no weapon to protect myself, I'd find a safe corner and stay there as long as I could. It's a normal reaction. But it doesn't get us anywhere.

Nevertheless, we just sit back and accept life as we've come to know it. This is especially the case for adults who were children of divorce. Until now, there has been no program specifically aimed at helping them with their issues stemming from the divorce. That's about to change with the Re-Right Your Past program, the adult version of Sandcastles.

Re-Right Your Past is a four-step program that you will follow in the next five weeks. It will be an intense five weeks, with lots of journal writing and reflecting on your past, starting with the earliest events that led up to your parents' divorce. However, the program doesn't really end when the formal part is over. The program's ultimate goal is to enable you to reach your full potential in life and let go of the stuff that's been holding you back. I say "stuff" because there is a lot of unresolved emotion in the baggage that constitutes your past.

During these five weeks you'll be visiting your past to prepare yourself for making meaningful change. It won't happen overnight. You'll undoubtedly experience a lot of mixed emotions, from feelings of satisfaction and elation to times of self-doubt and dissatisfaction. At times you might even feel despair. It's expected, because everyone goes through a variety of emotions when going through the program.

However, these five weeks are key because they take you through integral steps that will ultimately release the tight grip your parents' divorce has had and is having on your ability to go through life unencumbered by the insecurities that have been standing between you and where you truly belong. The steps will prepare you to sail onward on your own.

Getting Ready to Heal

Most likely you have vivid memories of what life was like before, during, and after your parents got divorced. You remember that the divorce affected you. You may recognize, on a conscious or an unconscious level, that it's still affecting you. Yet all these years you have worked to bury it. After all, what good is it to keep the memories and pain it caused front and center? Bad enough that it happened; do you have to have it hanging there every second of every day?

Now you're ready to do something different. You're ready to take action. This program will get you to stop burying the past by mentally going back to the point in time when it all started. There's no reason to hesitate. This time around you won't be traumatized. Rather, you'll find solace and comfort, because re-righting will show you how to use your past to understand how it has shaped your life and who you are today, and it will get you to the pivotal steps that will lead you to change and put you on the path of self-worth and personal satisfaction.

You will gain control over your life instead of being chained to your past, which more than likely has allowed you to bring too much trouble into your life. You will also realize there are many other people just like you who share the same feelings for the same reasons. You will be reading about their struggles and triumphs as you go through the program. Seeing that you are not alone, that your feelings are normal, is an important part of the process.

This Program Works!

This program has benefited others, and I am confident it will work for you as well.

Many of the same people who were so candid about their feelings in my survey also agreed to be part of my pilot study for the program. They received no more information than you are getting in this book. I never met them personally, and I have never counseled any of them. This was intentional, because I wanted to make sure this program could work for anyone through the use of the book alone, without personal counseling.

You'll be meeting many of these people throughout the book through their own words. Their words are real; the only thing I changed are their names in order to protect their privacy. You'll see examples of great success as well as great struggle—a real vision of what it means to change. As you'll see, there is no right or wrong, only genuine searching for understanding and finding your rightful place in life.

You Have the Power

I call the program Re-Right Your Past because I want to give you the image that you have the power to explore your issues and problems. Together we will fight the unfair and undeserved messages and painful feelings you endured in your youth that brought you to where you are today. If you are reading this book, you are clearly determined to make things better.

Many people are unaware of how dramatically their parents' divorce has negatively affected their lives. You might be thinking, "Not so. Believe me, Gary, I know I've been affected." However, once you start going through the program, you are likely to be surprised at how much more you have yet to realize. You'll begin to comprehend how your actions have been controlled by your childhood issues and then learn how to use these issues to finally take back control of your life. That's my goal. I want to help you complete the circle in which you end up changing your life, rather than getting stuck in a haze of sadness because we opened a Pandora's box. It's time for you to get proactive and gear up for genuine lasting change.

Re-righting is a highly interactive process that takes you on a positive path to meaningful change. It unfolds in four steps that will take you through the five weeks.

The Four Stages of Change
Step 1. Avoid Obstacles (Week 1)
The first step is crucial. We'll discuss all of the obstacles that can stop you from doing what is necessary to improve

your life. There are many tricks our minds play on us
that keep us from healing. In this step, you will learn to
avoid these obstacles so you can move on.

Step 2. Find Your Truth (Week 2)

The second week you'll be taking off the blinders and stepping back into your past. You'll face the whole messy
truth, learn to stop making excuses for the past and
defending people, and rewrite what really took place.

Step 3. Reflect Clearly on the Past (Week 3)

The truth leads you to see how your life developed into the
way you now live. In this step you will open your eyes
wide and let yourself realize how much your childhood
has dictated—yes, I mean *dictated*—the way you live.
You have actually been living on autopilot and process-
ing life based on a false idea of the truth. Now you will
come to terms with the effect that this false idea has had
on your life.

Step 4. Create Change in Your Life (Weeks 4–5)

Once you recognize that you are living life through the lens
of your childhood, you will finally possess the ability to
change. You will be able, on your own, to decide how you
want to approach life.

Reflecting on your childhood and the past events that have
led you to where you are today is imperative to make this program successful. This is why we are working through it slowly,
a week at a time. You need time for contemplation. However,
there is nothing sacred about the time frame. If a particular step
is hard for you, then you will need to take more time for it. It's
important that when you move on, you are ready to do so.
Similarly, with other steps you may think you've done your due
diligence after just a few days and be eager to move on. Feel
free to do so.

I've made step 4 two weeks long because change is hard. Yet the process is also ongoing; it doesn't necessarily occur on a time line, even two weeks rather than one, as though by magic. The fourth step is really the most time-consuming part of the program, in which you'll be doing a lot of contemplating and journal writing. You can't move through it too quickly if you want all the hard work that led up to it to stick. It is intended to make you sure-footed in the new understanding of who you really are, where you are going, and how you will interact with your environment. So I encourage you to take a minimum of two weeks for this step.

Get Ready to Write and Think

Re-Right Your Past is an interactive program, and you will be doing a lot of journal writing. So before you get started, find yourself a pen and a blank notebook that can be totally dedicated to this process. Make it something that is easy to write in, and keep the pen with it so it is conveniently in reach when you need to write.

Also find yourself a quiet place where you can be alone with your thoughts and do your journal writing. If necessary, inform those in your household that you will need some free and undisturbed time during the next five weeks. Ask that they respect your wishes and that no explanations be asked of you.

The Questionnaire

If you have this book in hand, you probably know that being brought up in a broken home can lead you to places you otherwise wouldn't have gone in life. There are lots of statistics that show that children of divorce get in more trouble in school, struggle academically, are more promiscuous as teens, are more likely to experiment with drugs and alcohol, and get in trouble with the law more than children raised in the traditional two-parent home. These types of issues, of course, follow you into adulthood. Their effect is real, but that's not what I'm dealing with in this book. You can't change your past, but you can make a better future for yourself, no matter what has been standing in your way.

Every day your mind makes decisions and takes action based on the emotional profile you developed starting as a child. It played a major role in shaping you into the person you are now. Most likely you're not content in life; you feel something missing. Perhaps your life is filled with too many disappointments. Maybe you're an underachiever and can't get yourself motivated. Maybe you are bad with money, struggle with relationships, have issues with fidelity, or are distrustful of others (or they are distrustful of you). Maybe you're just plain lonely and can't understand why. I could go on and on.

The point is that we all should have the opportunity to reach our full potential. Some of us just have more obstacles. The goal of this book is to get you to tear down your obstacles so there is nothing standing between you and what will give your life meaning.

With this in mind, I'd like you to take this quiz before you get started on the program. Answer each question yes or no. There's no score, no right or wrong answers. Just keep your answers as a reminder that these are things you *can* change and *will* change by going through the program.

Do you frequently feel sad or suffer from bouts
of depression?   Y   N

Do you suffer from anxiety?   Y   N

Are you divorced or middle-aged and never been
married?   Y   N

Do you worry that your own marriage might end
    in divorce, or are you avoiding marriage because
    you worry that it would end in divorce?   Y N

Do you worry that your spouse is cheating on you?   Y N

Do you have a problem sustaining close friendships? Y N

Do you have a problem finding or keeping a
    romantic interest?   Y N

Are you distrustful of love?   Y N

Do you have low self-esteem?   Y N

Do you lack self-confidence?   Y N

Do you have frequent feelings of guilt?   Y N

Do you have difficulty dealing with conflict?   Y N

Do you have trouble managing money?   Y N

Do you have fears about money?   Y N

Do you worry other people are taking advantage
    of you?   Y N

Do you anger easily or have fits of rage?   Y N

Do you think that your parents' divorce
    contributed to any of the questions you
    answered yes?   Y N

Note all the questions you've answered "yes" and write them in your notebook. They represent the part of you that is standing between you and where you want to go. So now let's get to work and get you to where you want to be in life.

PART 2

The Re-Right Your Past Program

3

Avoid Obstacles

Step 1, Week 1

Childhood is the time in which we learn about ourselves and how we fit into our world. Children must be nurtured in order to transition well into adults, and nurturing includes certain "musts." Think for a moment what these "musts" might be and create your list through the eyes of yourself as a child. Write it down in your journal.

What every child needs and deserves is _____.

When I ask adults to think about childhood in terms of need, the list of "musts" looks something like this:

- Unconditional love
- Warmth and affection
- Protection
- Words of affection
- Hugs and kisses

- Feeling valued
- Caring parents
- Stability
- Loving discipline
- Kindness

Now, take a look at these "musts" and those on your own list and consider what they say about childhood. I think you can sum them up with one word: dependence. Children are unable to be anything but dependent. As a child, you depended on others to supply your basic needs and help you navigate your world. As a child, you depended on these "musts" to develop emotional stability and give you a sense of security. They are of paramount importance in nurturing children to become healthy, loving, and emotionally secure adults.

When these "musts" are absent, it threatens your very sense of stability in an anxious, lost sort of way. It's like being unable to see in a dark room and tracing the walls in a helpless effort to find the exit. Imagine being a child in that dark room and finding the door, only to discover it doesn't lead to a safe haven. You're lost and on your own. Your very well-being is being threatened.

As an adult who was a child of divorce, you can probably relate to what I'm saying. Children of divorce feel loss on multiple levels. They feel alone in their anxiety, caused in part by knowing they're on their own in too many ways. The very nature of divorce doesn't allow for anything else. It's frightening for children to see the two people they love and depend on the most get caught up in their own distress or fighting. It puts the children in a dark place, feeling abandoned and left to manage on their own. It becomes part of their makeup.

You probably haven't given this much, if any, thought since you left home to be on your own. But it is at the core of where you are right now in life. It's also where you'll be going back to in this program. We'll be revisiting a lot of dark places, and it will be painful. So it is only natural to ask why.

Meet Reality

There are probably myriad thoughts going through your head right now telling you to stop this nonsense, have a drink, and use this book as a coaster. You can come up with many logical and sensible reasons not to bring up your parents' divorce and how you felt about it as a child. But these reasons are just a shield, a reaction to your fear that this program might be a waste of time.

Your hesitation is understandable. You have probably already tried to come to terms with the issues and conflicts in your life through counseling or with other self-help books, but neither worked. There's a reason they didn't work. Most psychological concepts are too broad to help an adult who was a child of divorce. This program is different because it is specific to you in this regard. It works because it gets you to come to terms with your issues by confronting your past—specifically, the events that surrounded your parents' divorce. It is really the only way for you to achieve real change.

Confronting the past is difficult because you have to overcome the conflicts that have been preventing you from doing so until now. These conflicts create obstacles, negatively charged excuses that always get in the way. They consume you with doubts and fears so strong that they can paralyze your desire for change. Getting over them is necessary for you to move forward.

We learn to avoid the obstacles by talking about them openly, keeping tabs on how they make us feel, and using our new understanding to push ourselves past them. That's what this first step is all about. It is so crucial to the success of this program that you're going to do nothing else this first week but come face-to-face with the fears that could hold you back.

I know what these obstacles are because I've heard people use them as excuses hundreds of times. They all have one thing in common: they touch on sensitive issues that involve you and your parents. Each one is legitimate and should not be minimized. In the next section are the five most common obstacles that create conflict for adults who were children of divorce. You may identify with all of them, a few of them, or just one. Maybe your obstacles are totally different. But don't fool yourself into thinking you don't have any. Everyone does.

For most of you, the five obstacles I describe here should tug at your consciousness in some way. I'll explain what each one is and why it's important that you overcome it. I'll show you how other people like yourself have responded to it. Then I will ask you to get out your notebook and respond to it yourself.

Fight the obstacles in your mind and get them down on paper. You will spend this week coming to grips with them and practicing avoidance. If at any time during this program you feel resistance or feel ready to quit, return to these pages in your journal.

Obstacle #1: I Don't Want to Be Disloyal

If I were to ask a group of people to quote something from the Bible that they knew word for word, I bet every person could quote one sentence without giving it much thought: "Honor thy father and thy mother." It is a basic tenet of religions as well as a necessary component of society. It says we must value our elders. We must be grateful to the two people who brought us into the world and worked tirelessly to care for us.

It's almost as though there were something sacred about parenthood that attracts unconditional loyalty from children. Think about yourself and your friends. Even if our parents screwed up big-time, it is still hard to trash them without feeling some discomfort or guilt about it. We can hate what they did, but we find it hard to hate *them*. This is an important thought to keep in mind, not just as you reflect on this obstacle but also throughout the program.

It is natural to be fiercely loyal to your parents. We especially hate it when someone else criticizes them. One of the classic images of a family feud is when one spouse says something negative about the other spouse's parent. There is something about hearing your spouse put down your parent that just rubs you the wrong way, even if you agree with your spouse. It is that deep-seated sense of loyalty and honor to defend your parents, no matter what.

Your Loyalty Talks Back

Of course, we realize that no parent is all good or all bad. Your conflicted mind says it's unfair to think of your parents critically because, after all, every parent makes mistakes. If you are a parent now yourself, you know how true this is. Being a parent is the hardest job in the world. Every parent struggles to do what's right for his or her children, and you know it wasn't so easy for your parents. It's why you always end up regretful after lashing out, or feeling like an ungrateful kid when you do or say something to hurt them.

Another nagging thought goes something like this: "My parents did a lot more things right than they did wrong. Why bring up a sore subject?" Of course, your parents did some wonderful things. It's good to remember and celebrate them for it. Parents *should* get credit for their efforts. But on the flip side, this doesn't mean that you should ignore their actions that shaped aspects of your life that you don't like. In fact, it's imperative that you don't ignore them.

Still, you might say, you don't want to go there, and it's unfair to them if you do. Think of it this way: Imagine a loving child approaching his or her parents and respectfully asking if it is okay to bring up part of the past so the child can heal from the lingering pain it is causing. Would a truly loving parent ask the child not to go there? I don't think so, and if your parents had only your best interest in mind, they'd agree.

It is this kind of loyalty that prevents you from thinking critically about your parents. You don't want to be disloyal. I'm telling you, however, that this kind of critical thinking does not constitute disloyalty.

Judge Actions, Not People

Your conflicted mind needs to know that there is a difference between judging people and judging actions. Judging your parents gets you into sensitive territory, which is why you should never go there.

It is unfair to judge your parents as individuals, because you can't fully understand what makes them tick and why they made the decisions in life that affected your life. Looking at what they did or didn't do that caused you heartache, however, is not labeling them as bad parents. Your logical mind needs to remind yourself that you are not being disloyal to your parents if you want to revisit the past. At no point in this process are you going to judge your parents. You are only going to judge how your parents' *actions* affected you.

A powerful personal example of judging actions versus people involves my grandfather, who passed away before I was born. I remember my father telling me that when he was a boy, my grandfather would punish him by hitting him with a sheaf of short leather strips made into a strap called a cat-o'-nine-tails. My grandfather kept the leather strap hanging on the wall for easy access—and as a reminder to my dad of what would happen if he crossed the line.

Should we judge my grandfather as a child abuser? After all, how dare he hit a child with such a tool as a way of discipline!

But before passing judgment, you need to know that every father in the neighborhood had a cat-o'-nine-tails hanging on the wall. My grandfather was simply providing discipline in the same way as everyone else in the neighborhood back then. It would be unfair to judge him apart from his society.

But this does not mean that the whippings didn't affect my father in some way. They did, no doubt. My father can judge what the experience did to him and how it shaped his life. Judging the method of punishment is not the same as judging the person who carried it out. If my father is critical of the whipping, he is not being disloyal to his own father.

Worry Is Just a Symptom

Worrying about being disloyal to your parents is part of the baggage that goes with being a child of divorce. As a child, you probably were anxious about loyalty issues. Children caught in the middle of divorce always worry about hurting their parents' feelings. For instance, they often don't want to tell Mom they'd like to spend more time at Dad's house for fear of hurting her. They don't want to tell Dad what a great time they had at Mom's (or with their stepfather) for fear of hurting him. This anxiety has followed you all of your life, and it's another reason you may feel conflicted now.

You may think that by stepping back to this uncomfortable time in your life, you are being disloyal to your parents. Just keep reminding yourself that you are not. In order to go forward, you are going to have to step back into an unhappier time in life, and you don't have to worry about anyone else's feelings but your own. In fact, your parents don't even have to know about it. At no time in this program will you be asked to confront your parents or share your feelings with them.

There is never any reason to be concerned about disloyalty. Fretting over it will only make you minimize events of the past and prevent you from getting in touch with your true feelings.

It could even suppress certain thoughts and memories that will be important to the healing process. You're on safe ground—you are not being disloyal.

....

SALLY'S STORY
She Feared Being Disloyal

Sally was always close to her mom but not her dad because she believed he was responsible for their divorce. She didn't realize that she had any issues with her mother until she started examining her past. Because she cared so much about her mom, she started feeling guilty about being disloyal. Here's what she had to say:

> I have always felt more comfortable telling my mom my feelings, since my dad always hurt my feelings. She has always been the nurturing and understanding parent. Lately, because I'm thinking about my past, I've been having feelings about her that I feel need to come out, but I am having trouble approaching her. When I try, she gets defensive and says, "How dare you, after everything I've done for you" or "I guess I failed as a parent, then, and I'm sorry you're all screwed up." There's no apology or any acknowledgment of where I'm coming from.
>
> I even approached my dad, and he just turns around everything I say and defends himself. I expected it from my dad, but not my mom. Neither wants to hear how much I have been hurt. They don't understand that I need them to be honest with themselves and me.

Sally speaks to the fact that you can avoid having insight in order to protect the image that you have about your parents. You might feel guilty and question yourself every step of the way. But if you want to change, the process begins by allowing yourself to search for your truth: how life was for you as a child and how it has affected you in reality. It can be a struggle, but it's a necessary one that is the key to changing your life.

Obstacle #2: I Don't Want to Feel Like a Victim and Just Blame Everything on My Parents

I know that psychology has left many people sour about looking into their pasts and their childhoods. Unfortunately, some mental health professionals get it wrong when they are trying to help someone create a different life through deeper insight.

They convince you that you are not the reason for your parents' divorce. Your parents are to blame. You are just the victim. This only leads you to a place of ambiguity that invites stuck thinking, such as "Well, I'm still messed up, but, whew, at least I'm not to blame." This achieves nothing. You are no more in control of your life than you were before. In fact, you're worse off, because you have been led to believe that you are paralyzed by your past, so strap yourself in and hold on tight for a roller-coaster ride through life.

This program isn't going in that direction. It doesn't lead you to recognize that your parents, not you, are the problem and then stop there. That's really only the start. But feeling like the victim is troubling to many people. It's an obstacle that stands in the way of getting to true healing.

It may be hard right now for you to envision how bringing up your childhood and your parents' behavior at the time will help you to gain control over your life. Trust me, we'll get there; that's a promise. I won't leave you hanging, just stuck with reliving feelings and memories that you've worked hard to forget. You'll get to the place in life that you deserve. To get there, however, you must look deeper within yourself. It's a step you can't skip.

The Blame Game

Excusing inappropriate behavior is a copout. Someone punches someone else because that person made him angry. A murder occurs because there's too much violence on television. You missed the breakfast meeting because the hotel alarm clock didn't work. All of these are really bad excuses.

You may be thinking, "If I blame my parents, am I saying that it's their fault I did the things I did to mess up my life? *I* did them. I don't want to palm my actions off on my parents, like some child." Well, guess what: that's the way you *should* feel. I am not asking you to relinquish control of your life or blame others for your decisions in the past. You and only you are responsible for yourself.

What you may not realize, however, is that the decisions you make are often based on very deeply encoded material in your memory. The code is drawn from your experiences as a child, and it is why you need to take a fresh look at these childhood experiences. You'll find as you continue that these life circumstances design your mental map: how you process your environment and take actions to live your life.

I am not asking you to blame your parents, nor am I trying to make you into a victim. I am asking you to allow yourself to review your life as candidly and truthfully as you can, without worrying about what it says or may say about you or your parents. How can you change without looking at as much truth as you can?

Defensiveness Is Easier Than Reality

It is natural to feel conflicted about seeing your parents' divorce as the source of your own personal struggles, as the following three journal entries attest. As you go forward, remember it was not your parents, it was their *actions*—the divorce—that is to blame.

Harriet has clearly struggled with the concept of blaming her parents, but now she shows a great "I will persevere" attitude. Here's what she wrote:

> I don't want to be a victim, and I don't want to blame my parents, but I am certainly not afraid of digging deep into my childhood. I see the value in it. I am trying to be clear around this, so it doesn't end up in some type of revenge. I never thought my life as it turned out was the doing of my parents' divorce, but I am seeing it—my lack of focus, clarity, financial success, and more. I am seeing it, but I will not stay paralyzed. I am willing to embrace this work and investigate and dig until I find my truth and true calling. At age fifty-one I know I am behind the eight ball, but I am healthy and have many great years ahead of me. I refuse to give up now.

For Sarah, her problem was her own failed relationships and her ongoing sense of distrust of anyone she loved. We will hear much more from Sarah later and see how the hurt of her childhood caused her to steer clear of looking back too much. She just wanted to avoid the pain, and not *blaming* her childhood was a good excuse to not *look* at her childhood. Here's what she wrote:

> I can't change what my parents did. I can only learn from it and promise myself I won't make those same mistakes—ever. So I don't have much interest in blaming them. In a way, I sort of disconnected myself from them the moment I realized that I was going to have to look out for myself,

since apparently they were fine with hanging me out to dry. Looking back at what they did does seem scary. I might get kind of angry with them. There are a lot of things they did that I don't truly understand, like why or how they could do the things that they did to their children. Yet I don't tend to blame them.

Cindy had a built-in excuse for her parents. Her way of minimizing her painful childhood was to find out why her parents behaved the way they did. Perhaps she is right about why they were unhealthy parents and that this can make her feel better about their truest intentions. But she can't use this to run away from the fact that their behavior was terribly painful, unfair, and uncalled for. It has left an indelible mark on her life. Understanding why her parents were the way they were doesn't change the pain she had to endure or the fact that she still needs to look back and understand what her childhood did to her. By saying her parents were raised by alcoholics, she's causing herself to feel guilty about blaming them for their unhealthy parenting. She needs to understand that even if they had a legitimate reason for hurting her the way they did, that doesn't minimize what that painful behavior did to her and how it affected her on a very core level. Here's how she expressed it:

I realize my parents are not perfect and they made mistakes. I just need them to be honest about themselves and admit they ignored my feelings because of their own selfish need to pretend everything was fine. My dad has moved on from the divorce, but my mom and I have not. It altered our entire life.

My parents had both grown up in alcoholic homes, and sometimes I think that maybe that could be why they messed up their own lives. Like they don't know how to express feelings, and they play guilt trips every time I try to tell them how I feel. Anytime I say something, they get defensive immediately. I can't fully blame my parents because I know they had been through their own difficulties as children, which shaped them to parent a certain way. For that I can forgive them.

Obstacle #3: I Don't Want to Hate My Parents and Find It Difficult to Be around Them

At the start of this program you will be bringing back the memories of your childhood and your parents' divorce, which may leave you vulnerable to a dangerous state of mind: feelings of anger toward your parents that can cross the line to hate.

The possibility of this may not be sitting well with you at the moment. Your conflicted mind might be saying, "My relationship with my parents may not be great, but it is what it is. I don't want to make it worse!" The last thing you want to do is make it difficult (or even more difficult, if it already is difficult) to be around them.

This kind of thinking creates an obstacle that may be especially hard to overcome if either one of your parents has passed away, because you don't want to tarnish his or her memory. "Leave well enough alone," your mind says.

I assure you, I am not going to take you to a place you don't want to go and leave you stranded there. You're going to have some anger; it's part of the process. But remember, it is not directed at them, it's directed at the situation. This work is not about blame, it's about change. It's not about getting trapped in anger. Rather, you will work through the anger, and you'll end up in a better, more sincere relationship with them or a calmer place within if they've passed on. That in itself should make it all worthwhile.

Your conflicted mind may argue that you have a good relationship with both of your parents, even if one relationship is better than the other. "Why risk wrecking it?" you ask. Or you may be reticent about embarking on this program because you fear that the process will trigger some awful memory that will infect your relationship with one or both of your parents. Well, guess what: your relationship is already infected. Even if it is unspoken or filed away in your memory, there is stuff about your parents and childhood sitting there, decaying, infecting your relationship with Mom and Dad. No matter what kind of relationships you have with your parents, they could be better. Much better. And they will be.

That's really the message of this book. Hiding from the issues doesn't make them go away or stop them from interfering in your life. Trust me, when you have completed this program, you will feel much better about any issue you previously had with your parents.

Imagine it this way. Let's say you were playing softball and someone on the other team—a friend, in fact—got angry with you and, in the heat of things, punched you in the nose. Ten years later, you see that person in a restaurant. How do you react? Well, it depends. If the punch broke your nose and it's been a problem for you ever since, just seeing this guy could make you angry enough to want to hit him on the spot. But if the punch created only short-term pain and inconvenience, then you might be willing to nod or shake his hand.

This program gets you above it all. It's not about anger or revenge. It's about moving on. You're going to experience some pain and anger, but it will not fester. You just need to remind yourself to stay in motion.

The Discomfort Will Only Be Temporary

Moving forward is likely to complicate your relationship with your parents, but it will be temporary. Throughout the program you are going to experience the memories and fears of your childhood all over again. You may be surprised to find out how raw they still can be. However, you're not going to fight them; you're going to face them. As a result, you're going to get angry and aim some of that anger at your parents.

There may be times during this process when you'll want to avoid your parents a bit, or you may find it harder to be around them. You will need to be careful. In other words, you don't want to be picking a fight at the Thanksgiving dinner table because you are in the process of remembering and feeling certain childhood emotions. There is no place for venting in this book.

Remember, as awkward as seeing your parents during this program may be at times, the process itself is necessary to achieve the ultimate goal of healing and changing your life. In the end, you are likely to have an even better relationship with your parents, because you will have resolved much of your pain.

Taking part in this program will not put you at any risk of ruining any part of your relationship with your parents. We will remain acutely aware of this during the entire process. I will be very clear as we go along that you will not be using the work we do to engage in conversation with your parents, unless you have thought it through properly. This is so important that chapter 8 is devoted to the topic of how to interact with your parents. For some of you, it is not going to be worthwhile to have *any* conversation with them about this. If you choose to, however, you will be armed with plenty of information and techniques to make the conversation have a healthy, desired outcome.

The key to having a better relationship with your parents is to face the hurt your parents caused you by getting divorced and pretending it away. You will have a better, more manageable, more sincere relationship with your parents if you do the work to heal. In the end, you will be able to say to yourself, "Okay, there were certain hurtful things and mistakes you made, Mom or Dad. But I've healed, and they don't affect my life in a negative way anymore." You will have a newfound ability to interact with your parents and think about them without feeling hurt, pain, or anger. Once you've healed, you can more easily focus on the positive aspects and develop a relationship or a memory that is not full of hurt and sadness.

I can't promise that in the end you'll have a *perfect* relationship with your parents. However, you will have a more sincere and honest one. You'll have a deeper understanding of each other. Best of all, you'll be able to *choose* how you want to relate to your parents.

Putting Your Parental Relationship in Focus

If you're worried that digging up old wounds will hurt your relationship with your parents, consider this: your relationship has been damaged for so long it just feels natural. Realizing this will put your relationship in better focus. These two journal entries are very typical of how adults who were children of divorce view their relationship with their parents when they can admit it only to themselves:

> It can't get any worse. Yes, I'd say to this, true, true, true. So I really don't have a ton of worries about this obstacle. It's already difficult to be around my parents, so I'm used to it. It just is.
>
> —Andrea

> I have both of my parents in my life today, and we got through life as if everything is normal. But to be honest, I do avoid them when I have feelings

of sadness or anger for them. They also avoid me if they sense any sort of feelings like that from me. Every time I have those feelings I hold it in around them, but the feelings always find a way to come out in passive-aggressive behavior. For me, that's normal. But it really isn't, is it?

—Louise

Obstacle #4: Seeing My Parents' Mistakes Will Make Me Judge My Own Parenting Skills

It can sometimes be scary to wonder what our own children might say about us a decade or two from now. When you start to investigate your own childhood to see what your parents did or didn't do to you, you're probably going to start judging your own parenting behavior: "Am I doing the same thing to my kids?!" It's almost guaranteed to happen.

But think a moment. It's not such a bad thing to look at yourself from this perspective, is it? After all, imagine if your parents had only done the same thing way back when. Things just might be a lot different today!

Beware of Detours

It's important for you to confront the truths about yourself, even if it means seeing yourself in ways that are not so positive. Maybe you do see a little of your parents in your attitude toward your own children. It can be painful to think about, but denying it or hiding it only means you're more likely to continue to do so. Recognizing it and correcting it, however, makes you a better person *and* a better parent. Even if your children are adults, don't think it won't make a huge difference to them if you suddenly recognize some of your parenting errors, apologize, and attempt to discuss it with them. It would go a very long way in their own healing and ability to make their lives better.

There is an inherent problem in involving yourself in this right now, though, because it can thwart your current goal of healing yourself and changing your life. The goal right now is not to make you a better parent; rather, it's to make you a healthier person who can live up to your full potential. Parenting is, of course, part of it, but I must caution you not to allow yourself to get consumed with self-doubt about your own parenting skills. Taking the focus away from your primary goal would be a major pitfall. For example, sometimes people use their own parenting mistakes as a way to minimize their childhood hurt. It's like saying, "That was hurtful, but look what I do, so it isn't that bad."

If you come to realize that you too bring unnecessary pain to your kids, it is something that you definitely need to address. Just don't allow the concerns about your parenting style to stop you from seeking the truth about your childhood now.

Parental Self-Doubt Is Common

At some point, all parents question their parenting skills. For adults who were children of divorce, there are always doubts, because they didn't really have a role model—at least in the traditional sense. These two journal entries are great examples and, I might add, very typical:

> Ha ha, just reading about how I think I have failed my children gives me guilt. Whew! So glad you are bringing this one up. . . . Maybe there is hope yet that my girls will turn out to be "normal" instead of questioning life, acting out, and trying to get attention, sometimes in the most dangerous of ways! Okay, I will not get detoured by my fear of my

own parenting. When I start to avoid this program because it's starting to feel like I'm a bad parent, I'll catch myself and remember this is normal for everyone going through this program, and that will force me to stay on task. I won't explain away what my parents did by saying I'm just as bad. Now I can see that I could be using that to avoid doing this.

—Joanna

Sure, I carry this fear around about parenting, and I don't even have kids yet! I do think about things I would do differently when I do get to that point in my life. It is a big fear for me that I might get hurt by my future husband and damage our future children like I have been hurt by my parents. I am the happiest in life when my parents are talking as good friends together, and it is such a great feeling being in their presence together as a family unit. Obviously that's not what usually happens, so instead I'm left with worry that I'll be a terrible parent ultimately. I have to put this out of my mind as I go through this and stop saying, "Who knows what kind of horrible parent you'll be?" as a way to let my own parents off the hook.

—Rene

Obstacle #5: I Don't Know Anything Different

We've all heard about people who forgot about horrors that happened to them as children and then had them shockingly emerge in their memories years later. Sometimes psychologists are looking for the worst, which can lead patients to exaggerate the past, but that's not what's going on here.

In this process, you will not be looking for an "aha!" moment that brings it all into perspective and explains everything. You are looking for what really happened and, most important, how it felt to be you under those circumstances. You already know what messed up your life or put strife in it: everything surrounding your parents' divorce. However, it is a common concern among many that the process of recall I am asking you to go through may elicit more fiction than fact. That is, you'll be making stuff up. There is some truth in this, but not in the way you might think.

Recalling scenes—a major fight, the moment you learned about the divorce, or when your dad moved out—isn't the issue. What you might have difficulty doing is recalling your exact feelings at that time.

Memory is tricky. You can recall an incident and think you really didn't feel hurt or frightened by it. For example, you can remember a particularly bad fight your parents had, but you don't necessarily remember how it ended, what it was about exactly, or how it started. You might not recall how you felt, or you might recall not having felt sad at all.

Hilda, who was in my research group, is a true-life example. She told me that her parents had horrendous fights in which they'd scream at each other and throw things. She said she couldn't recall feeling sad or scared because every time her parents fought, she ran to her room and drowned it out by listening to her favorite music on a headset. She didn't feel upset because she hid from the incident. However, she was hiding her feelings, and these were as real as what was going on in the other room.

I asked Hilda how she came to use this coping strategy. She assumed that there had been earlier incidents in which her parents yelled at each other and that this had been awful for her. Clearly, the fighting had to have been often and upsetting enough that she developed a way to put her thoughts and hearing elsewhere.

Is she making up stuff? Not at all. Since it was normal that her parents fought constantly, she emotionally checked out and didn't stand there crying or trying to break it up, as some children often do. You could say she has no memory of being pained about it at all—her coping mechanism was that good. She knew nothing else her whole childhood. Yet it's unlikely that she *never* felt bad about it. You have to assume that sometime earlier, she had had an emotional reaction to her parents' vicious fighting and that this drove her to invent a coping strategy.

But we can also assume something else for Hilda: that there was a negative effect. Perhaps that effect wasn't depression, but as Hilda discovered while going through this program, it was her consistent ability to check out of life and recede from any confrontation. It made her marriage impossible; since she couldn't manage any moment of tension between her and her husband, it caused her to have a very superficial relationship with him.

Just that one insight gave Hilda the ability to learn to manage conflict and stay put in her marriage, instead of running away from it as she had run from her feelings since her childhood. She allowed herself to recognize that she went into her own world because she was sad. She also recalled something she had forgotten: that she would take off the headset every few minutes to listen if the yelling had stopped. In the end she recognized that sadness was attached to the whole event.

A New Look at Reality

In this process, you will be going after any emotional effect your childhood has had on you. In order to recognize your genuine emotions, you will need to take a fresh look at some things through a different lens. It is common for families to try to minimize past family events by turning them into something they were not. In Hilda's case, the events of childhood were eventually turned into amusing family lore. For years, when Hilda and her brother got together with her mother or her father, they'd laugh about the fights and how she and her brother would always pick up their favorite breakable objects before leaving the room so their parents wouldn't throw them at each other and break them.

One time, her parents had smashed a lamp made out of Popsicle sticks that her brother had made. That was recalled as funny, only Hilda came to realize that there was nothing humorous about it at all. Over time, the family managed the painful moments by laughing about them, but this is just a coping technique. It didn't mean there was no pain.

Going forward, you'll have to take a hard new look at everything, even those pieces of life you've come to explain to yourself as the norm. Normal isn't always reality.

....

BRENDA'S STORY
A "Normal" Way of Thinking

This obstacle was a particularly thorny one for Brenda. Read how she expressed it in her journal:

> Okay, this is an obstacle that makes me nervous. My "normal" may be kind of sucky and awful, but it's still "normal" and much less scary than the unknown. The thought of making things better and being happy sounds like a great idea, but it's also a scary idea. I mean, who knows when that could be snatched away?
>
> The fear of fixing things and then having it be taken away is worse than just staying with things the sad way they are. (And, yes, I do know how warped that is.) Yet I know that if I stay at my current level of "normal," I won't ever get what I want: to be happy,

to have a husband and children, to actually live life and not just try to survive. So even though trying to change sounds uncomfortably scary, I can't let that deter me from trying to make a new normal.

I've always kind of thought that I'm good at putting things in perspective. At work my famous line when something goes wrong is "Well, no one is dead." When something bad happens, my coworkers will look at me and say, "Say it!" I guess it comes from the thought process I used when my parents were getting a divorce. I mean, I still had both parents. They might not be together, but they were still alive, and I could talk to them if I wanted to. It would have been worse if one of them had died. I had no right to complain.

All things considered, I had it good. Yet here I sit almost paralyzed, frozen in time for something that I think I can easily talk myself out of thinking. Is that such a big deal compared to other possible things that could go horribly wrong? Or, maybe it just helps me to pretend that it's not really a big deal. I think I need to know to be aware of this as I move forward.

To Brenda, the idea of change is just plain scary. It is a normal human reaction. We are used to life as it is, and even though we know it isn't giving us what we want, we still know how to navigate it and manage. To change, we have to see our past for what it really was, not the "normal" our family made us believe it was. However, just because we were made to believe it was normal doesn't make it so.

This is a complex issue, because we've come to define so much in life based on what we were taught. Our moral code and so much more are developed in our youth. Realizing that what we grew up feeling and believing might be suspect and may need to change can make anyone anxious.

But having the courage to question it all, as Brenda is doing, helps to create a new sense of what is truly healthy for you and will lead you to live the life you've always wanted. The upside is making a life for yourself of your choosing and developing a new and healthy belief system.

....

Journal Time

Now it's your turn. It's time to reckon with these obstacles. Take a few days to ponder them:

1. I don't want to be disloyal.
2. I don't want to feel like a victim and just blame everything on my parents.
3. I don't want to hate my parents and find it difficult to be around them.
4. Seeing my parents' mistakes will make me judge my own parenting skills.
5. I don't know anything different.

Think about them in terms of your own life. Then find quiet time and start writing. Write about each one of them. Even if you believe that none of the five obstacles pertain to you, ask yourself why not and respond in writing. You might be surprised that you're really just deluding yourself. That's the thing about obstacles. They can be invisible but come at you stealthily with the power of a Mack truck when you least expect it. So you want to be prepared.

I would also like you to spend this week reflecting on other obstacles that could be holding you back. Write down what they are and then reckon with them. Talk to yourself about these concerns and try to resolve them. Just writing about them and seeing them in front of you can dispel them enough to help you move on.

If, as you go forward, you start feeling overwhelmed and obstacles start getting in the way, come back to these pages in your journal. Reviewing your original responses to your obstacles can reinforce your effort to stay with the program. Revisit these concerns at any time and evaluate whether they have been resolved or are still causing you concern.

Again, writing your internal dialogue is crucial to this process. It'll help you see your changes and improvements and will greatly assist you in developing the new you. We may need to revisit feelings and thoughts many times to better understand them. No matter how repetitive something seems, write it down and let it become part of the process.

4

Find Your Truth

Step 2, Week 2

Truth is a puzzling thing. Two people can be standing in the same place and witness the same action, yet they can have two completely different sets of thoughts and feelings about what they saw.

For example, let's say two women are waiting at a traffic light when a bus stops to drop off and pick up passengers. One woman watches as a young mother clasps the hand of a child carrying a balloon and gets on board. She thinks, "How sweet. They must be going to a party." The other bystander just stares at the black smoke coming from the bus's exhaust and takes in the odor of diesel fuel. All she can think is "Get this bus out of here!"

Same scene, two different perspectives. If you were to use this example to draw a conclusion about life, you would have to say that one person sees life as an opportunity and the other sees it as toxic.

Your sense of truth about your life depends on your perspective. Do you view life as an opportunity, or do you think it's toxic? Or do you see it somewhere in between? Being an adult who was a child of divorce can mean you've had a life filled with disappointment and missed opportunities, because a skewed perspective has tainted it. Your perspective on life is built on a foundation of childhood experiences. And, as you know, a childhood consumed by the dysfunction of a broken family can take you to some dark and scary places. Understanding the early emotions that formed your perspective—that is, the truth about your childhood—is what you'll be working on this week. You will be searching for the truth by piecing together your childhood and the events surrounding your parents' divorce.

It certainly sounds like a daunting task, but I will walk you through it step-by-step, and you'll also have the guidance of others who have been in the same situation. To help you bring your childhood memories forward, I offer you samples of different memories from those who have experienced the Re-Right Your Past program, including a fuller example at the end of this chapter. I hope they will assist you in remembering and recording your own memories.

So be patient, read this chapter, and then get out your pen and journal. This is your week for re-creating your past.

How Your Past Determines Your Truth Today

You are likely to know intuitively that your parents' divorce has affected the way your life has unfolded. What you may not realize is how profoundly the divorce has affected you. Images and feelings stored away in your brain are the key to understanding how your past has followed you through life and how it is affecting you today.

The brain is an amazing organ. Brain-imaging studies have shown that a person of average intelligence processes between fifty and seventy thousand thoughts every day. The brain is also a highly efficient organ. It takes about 90 percent of these thoughts and either filters them or sends them to the recesses of your memory. You can prove this to yourself rather easily the next time you cross a busy street. You stop, look right, then left (and maybe right again), and then your brain gives you the signal to either cross or wait.

Simple, right? Yet if you were able to see this process in slow motion, you might be surprised to realize how many thoughts are involved in making that momentary decision. When you looked in each direction, your brain did incredibly fast work. You thought about the approaching traffic and how fast the vehicles were going. In order to do this, your brain had to signal your vision to take a series of snapshots in a matter of milliseconds in order to judge how quickly the traffic was moving, moment by moment.

At the same time, your brain signaled your sense of sound to listen for the noise of approaching traffic to determine how close it was and how fast it was heading in your direction. You did this in both directions in just seconds. You then made a mathematical hypothesis that it was safe to cross the street, a judgment based on how fast traffic was approaching versus the speed at which you could cross the street safely. (And you think you aren't good at math?)

In that split second, you may have made several different mathematical calculations, from crossing at your typical walking speed to walking briskly to making a run for it. At the same time that all of this was going on in your head, the intuitive center in your brain was checking out the traffic light and scanning the curb to judge what other people were doing. It all occurs in less time than it just took for you to read about it!

Imagine how many mathematical determinations you make when driving a car. When you think of it from this viewpoint, your brain's job is overwhelming! The brain is always in drive—it is "on" continuously, even when you are just lying around. That's why the brain needs to be an efficient organ with a good filtering system. It is programmed to do this intense kind of thinking and reacting without you having to be fully aware of the blow-by-blow sequence required to form a thought.

In many ways, the brain is a lot like a computer. Most of us really don't understand what's going on in the hard drive that allows our computers to respond to all our commands. When it's working well, we're content, and we don't have to concern ourselves with how the computer functions. When it doesn't do what we expect it to do—well, we all know what that is like. We get frustrated, then frantic. We might even feel like we're falling apart because of how much we depend on our computers in our day-to-day lives.

It's the same with the brain. The "computer chip" in your brain is continually alert for new commands. When it's not responding well—when life is repeatedly not working out to your satisfaction—you're left in a quandary, clueless about how to fix it.

Unfortunately, you can't buy a newer model of brain the way you can buy a new computer. The only way to correct what's wrong with your life is to figure out why your brain is driving you to act and respond the way you do. You could seek the help of a therapist, but if you're like most people, you think you can figure it out and fix it yourself. So you might work on your love life or your parenting skills, or you might start looking for a new job—whatever you think will get you on the right course to happiness. In reality, it's a lot of work, and, at best, all you are doing is reducing the symptoms. You're not curing the problem. This program is going to cure the problem.

A friend shared with me a funny computer metaphor for this concept. Imagine that you write a letter on the computer and print it out. When you look it over, you see a typo, so you scratch it out on the paper and print a new copy. The same typo appears. This time you get some white-out fluid, correct the mistake, and print the letter again. As you know, this still isn't going to work, because you're going about it all the wrong way. In order to fix the problem, you have to go back to the computer, open the document, delete the error, and replace it with the correct letter. The same goes for the mistakes you make in life. In order to get on the right course, you have to go to your computer (your brain), open the document (your memory), and find the mistake (how you were made to feel) before you're able to fix it.

Is Your Life on Autopilot?

Although we don't realize it, most of us go through our day-to-day lives on autopilot. Don't misunderstand; I am not implying that we are aimlessly going through life. It's just that we have programmed ourselves to think and respond in a typical way within our own comfort zone. Just as in an airplane cockpit, autopilot is not haphazard; it has to be programmed. *You* have been programmed on your path in life. It's what I call your *mental map*.

Naturally, we think that we each set our own life course, but we really don't—we can't. That's because autopilot requires a set of tools and dials to set the program. These tools and dials are our life experiences, and they start shaping our mental maps the moment we are born. Even though it's something we rarely (if ever) think about, we enter this world aware of only one biological necessity: to be cared for. Your mental map started programming your life right from the start. Every—yes, *every*—event you have experienced since birth played a role in the mental map that set your autopilot. It's not something we are consciously aware of, yet we are constantly using that map to think, evaluate, and define our lives: "This is just who I am."

You might say you're the kind of person who's sad, lazy, confused, guilt-ridden, shy, unattractive, not stylish, underachieving, unlucky at love, hot-tempered, weak, undeserving, unworthy, unaccomplished, antisocial, irresponsible, procrastinating, not very healthy, not good with money, or not a very attentive parent. Or you might say you're just the opposite, the kind of person who is upbeat, happy-go-lucky, clearheaded, genuine, outgoing, athletic, attractive, in a great relationship, calm, strong, deserving of great things, accomplished, sociable, responsible, dependable, in great shape, good at making and managing money, or an awesome parent. Most likely you have some traits from both lists.

These traits that describe you as a human being come from your mental map, the composite of your life experiences. And the original architects of your mental map are your parents, the people responsible for supplying you with your first biological need to be cared for.

The Mental Map of a Child of Divorce

Your parents played a major role in developing your mental map because they were your lifeline to the world. As a child you depended on them for everything. They managed your life. Even as you grew into a teen and started to take responsibility and challenge their authority, your parents were still largely calling the shots. They were defining your mental map, or setting your autopilot.

So how does a mental map work for a child of divorce? Witnessing your parents' fighting and living through their divorce as a child could have made you shy and fear confrontation. Make no mistake, the divorce had everything to do with why you might have felt unworthy of the attention of your tenth-grade heart-throb, even after he or she pursued *you*. It's also why you might have stayed in a relationship with a college boyfriend or girl-friend who wasn't particularly nice to you and with whom you really didn't have much in common.

This is not an oversimplification. Your parents' divorce played a leading role in shaping your mental map and taking you to where you are in life today.

Change Your Autopilot

At one time, scientists believed that the brain was hardwired at birth, but they now know this is not the case. The relatively new science of neuroplasticity shows that the brain is highly mallea-ble and has the remarkable ability to rewire its circuits and form new connections. In short, you can "re-right" your mental map.

Right now your mental map is like a GPS gone amok that insists you take a lot of needless or wrong turns. It makes no sense to continue to use it, yet in life that is exactly what you do, over and over. After a while, you find yourself with so many prob-lems you really do begin to feel utterly lost.

The good news is that you don't have a thousand problems; you have one, and it's causing a thousand symptoms. Attacking the symptoms is simply too hard and time-consuming, and it isn't going to solve your problem. So let's get to the root of the problem: the events before, during, and after your parents' divorce. Seeing these events as they truly are is the first major step in resetting your autopilot and getting you on the road to change. Once you're there, you'll be able to resolve, heal, and deal with all of the symptoms at once.

Remake Your Memories

What you will be doing in this step is seeking the truth. Not the "truth" you were made to believe as a child, not the "truth" you were fed by your parents, but the truth as it really was and is. Children are very impressionable and absorb whatever messages they receive. Unfortunately, these impressions are like a permanent-ink pen in your memory, telling a story out of sync with reality.

For example, a common misconception of many adults who were children of divorce is the belief that they were difficult kids. In most instances, this was really not the case. However, when you're constantly being given the impression that you are flawed in some way, you start to believe it. What kind of way is that to start out life?

One story I found particularly sad came from a young man in my research group whom I'll call Robert. He told me that as a kid, he was always embarrassing his mother. He recalled an instance when he played the piano for his mother and some friends she was entertaining at home. "I was pretty good for being only five, but I was nervous and messed up a couple of notes really badly," Robert recalled. "My mom told me later she was so embarrassed she could never invite her friends back. When they didn't come back, I figured it was because of my playing."

To compound Robert's guilt was the fact that his dad was an accomplished musician. When his dad walked out on the family two years later, Robert was convinced that his lousy piano playing and lack of study had disappointed his dad and driven him away. It didn't matter that his mother had always had difficulty maintaining friendships and that his dad was running around with another woman. Finding this out years later did little to assuage Robert's guilt, because he was convinced he was a lazy child. In his own words, he was "hard to take."

Through this program, Robert began to see a new truth with his adult eyes. He was able to recall how horrible he had felt whenever he heard his mother screech because he hit a wrong chord on the piano. If he practiced an hour a day, his mom said it wasn't good enough. If he practiced two hours a day, that still wasn't good enough. He was led to believe that he was a problem child when in fact he was showing potential as a musician. He grew up loving the piano, but he'd never play for anyone.

When he faced the truth about the events that surrounded his parents' divorce, he realized he was just his mother's emotional punching bag. The truth was that he was a pretty wonderful child and could have become a professional musician. This program gave Robert the clarity to return to the piano. Renewing his acquaintance with the music he had always loved was his way of bringing back his past with clearer insight. The piano became instrumental in his ability to heal and change. He regained his confidence and today has a piano in his home that he plays almost daily.

The moral of this story brings me to the all-important rule of finding the truth: Avoid your parents' viewpoints of your memory. Stick with the truth as best *you* know it. Instead of "I was a really tough kid, so my mom spanked me with a Ping-Pong paddle," the truth might be more like "I was five and had to go to the bathroom. I couldn't wait and peed in the car. Mom was so mad she got out the Ping-Pong paddle. Just the sight of it made me cry hysterically."

Now it's time for you to begin to find the truth. Writing about your memories is a very important first step in re-righting your life. Recalling your memories will take some time, so give yourself a few days to think about them before you begin to write. Try to come up with ten to twelve memories from your childhood that relate to your parents' divorce. Allow each memory to unfold in three steps:

1. *This is the full memory as best I can recall.* Write it down as it comes to you. Do not try to edit it or make it sound better. It's important to see it as it flows from your brain.

2. *This is how I felt at the time.* As you write down the memory, you will probably also remember the emotion you went through at the time. What was it? How do you recall feeling at the time this event took place? If you can't remember, then try to imagine how a child in that situation is likely to feel.

3. *This is how I feel now as I write it down.* How do you feel as you recall the memory? Are you reliving the feeling you recall having had at the time, or do you feel something different? What is your current interpretation of the memory?

Try to remember the entire time surrounding your parents' divorce: before their separation, during the period of separation, and after the divorce. All of these time elements are important.

·············· MEMORIES ··············

Holidays Are Tough

Sadness around holidays, especially Christmas, shows up in virtually everyone's top ten memories. Many adults who are children of divorce tell me that they don't seem to enjoy Christmas as other people do. Unpleasant memories, such as this one from James, are the reason.

This is the full memory as best I can recall: "This is one of my most profoundly sad memories. I'm ten, and it is Christmas morning. My twelve-year-old sister and I had tons of gifts, and the four of us were sitting around the tree opening them. The whole time the thought going through my head was 'This is our last Christmas as a family.' I had absolutely no pleasure from the gifts and the holiday—just horrible fear and grief."

This is how I felt at the time: "Heartbroken and afraid to share my feelings. I was worried all of the time. I did not feel like I could share my concerns with them. I was afraid if I mentioned anything, the divorce would become a reality, even though I knew there was no way it would *not* happen."

This is how I feel now as I write it down: "Sad that I had to go through all this, that I had to be constantly nervous and filter my words throughout most of my childhood."

································ MEMORIES ································
A Shattering Secret

This memory comes from Bob. It's a pivotal point in his life because learning about the possibility of divorce left him nervous and on edge. He was so scared about it that he kept it private. Now as an adult he can appreciate the profound effect the anxiety in his home had on him, and then the worst-case scenario coming true.

This is the full memory as best I can recall: "When I was probably about seven years old I remember going through boxes in our basement and finding a letter that was from my mom to my dad. It had been written a few years earlier and it said she wanted a divorce."

This is how I felt at the time: "I was confused yet glad that it never came to fruition—at least it hadn't at that point. I did hear my parents fight often, so this did concern me. I put it back and never said a word, as if keeping this 'secret' would prevent it from ever happening."

This is how I feel now as I write it down: "It makes me kind of sad to think of that little boy sitting in the basement reading that letter and always being on edge that it might happen—that my parents would divorce and my life would completely change."

································

Writing Down Your Memories

Your journal is instrumental to successfully completing this step. You'll be writing a lot this week, so consider your journal part of you. You will be recalling all of the memories you can capture of the time before, during, and after your parents' divorce and writing them down. I'd like you to remember every scene. This may seem like a difficult task at first, but one memory will trigger another, and that one will bring back yet another. So stick with it.

Re-righting is about digging deep, and writing down memories is the beginning. Don't be intimidated or worried about your writing ability. Nobody is going to read it but you. It's *what* you write that counts, not how you write it. You'll also have plenty of help from me and others like yourself. Below you'll find tips that will guide you each step of the way, followed by sample true-life journal entries from people who have already successfully completed the program.

Shoot for ten memories. Your goal is to write down all of your memories, but for starters I'd like you to go back to your top ten memories. There is nothing magical about the number ten, but anything less won't be as productive. The more, the better, for it will help you to piece together how your personality was developed.

Prepare your journal. Mark the section "Finding Truth" and leave at least a page for each memory. Start each memory on a new page so you have room to go back and add to it as new snippets come to mind. Label the pages Memory 1 through Memory 10. Here are some tips to help get you started:

- *It's all about the divorce.* When recording your memories, relate them to the divorce as best you can. If you can't recall ten memories that involve the time surrounding the divorce, go on to other memories involving any time of childhood.

- *Start out easy.* Begin with the memories that are obvious, the ones you can't help but remember. For example, most people remember when, where, and how they were told that their parents were splitting up. Write as you remember. Don't edit any of it. Start with the memories you've told others about before, then move on to those you haven't told anyone about.

- *Consider your feelings.* This is the key component of this exercise. As you are writing your memories, recall how you felt then and consider how you are feeling now. Write "How I felt then" and "How I feel now" each on a line of its own. If any feelings change, make sure to record them.

- *Expect intense emotion.* This program is designed to evoke a lot of emotion in a short amount of time. You need to feel these old emotions intensely. It is a necessary component of the process. You must start to realize how your life has been dictated by your childhood. If you work on this every day for a week, the feelings of each memory will begin to link to one another and you'll begin to get a fuller view of what your life was like as a kid.

- *Put the stress on early memories.* Everyone has an easier time remembering his or her teenage years than early childhood years. As you'll learn later, by the time adolescence occurs, your personality is already largely formed. Ideally, you want to try to remember earlier memories, since they will help you to understand how your personality was shaped. This doesn't mean that an adolescent memory won't be helpful. Write it down, too, but be sure to think back to as young as you can recall.

- *Bits and pieces are valuable.* Write down even bits of scenes as you can recall them. Keep in mind that you don't need to remember an event in its entirety for it to be valuable. If you can only remember overhearing your parents yelling about getting a divorce, but you can't remember who was with you or even exactly where you were at that moment, it is still a crucial memory.

- *Remember the bad and the good.* You're likely to start out by recalling the bad stuff, but try to think about the good times as well. You can learn a lot about yourself from your good memories. There won't be many of these associated with the divorce itself, but you may remember the thrill of finally seeing your parent after a long separation or what it was like to have both parents attend your graduation or school play.

- *Block out writing time.* You can't expect to do a task like this all at once. Use the full week to work on it. I suggest you block out thirty minutes to an hour once or twice a day to do your journal writing. This should be uninterrupted time. You don't want to be rushed because it will limit your willingness to fully feel the emotions. You can't experience old feelings if your kids are knocking on the door needing your immediate attention. Also, there is a saturation point, when you need to stop focusing on the raw feelings that are likely to make you sad. When the time is up, don't dwell. Move on.

- *Decompress.* Reminiscing this way can be emotionally moving, making you moody or bringing you to tears. If possible, plan to write at a time when you can also plan for some decompression time afterward. This could include taking a hot bath, going for a brisk walk or a jog, reading a book, taking a drive, or relaxing in any way you enjoy.

- *Don't be hard on yourself.* Be kind to yourself during this experience, just as you'd be kind to a loved one who was going through this process.

- *Warn others.* Rehashing the past and bringing up bad memories will have an effect on your mood. Ideally, you should let other adults who are close to you or who live with you know that you may be a little down at times. However, I suggest that you don't share this with young children in your household. You need to be there for them, not the other way around.

- *Don't let excuses get in the way:* Remember, as much as you want to change, obstacles can convince you to put this off. Don't allow yourself to fall for mental excuses.

- *Make this an ongoing process.* If you work diligently this week, you will be able to recall dozens of stories and bits of memories. It's important that you get the bulk of your memories down before moving to step 3. However, consider this an ongoing process. Add memories as they come to you, whether it's during the formal part of the program or afterward. It's likely that you will find this process so liberating that you'll want to continue writing down your memories far into the future.

·············· MEMORIES ··············
The Price of Secrecy

This is another common theme: Children have worries about their parents' divorce yet are afraid to talk about it with anyone. They think their friends will see and treat them differently. It is one of the primary reasons I developed the Sandcastles program; I wanted children to share their feelings with other children and to feel better from having shared them. Jared's responses to the prompts illustrate this problem.

This is the full memory as best I can recall: "One day, I was sleeping over my friend Tommy's house and we were just hanging out in his backyard. His mom had made us these ice cream sundaes, and we were eating them and comparing baseball cards. This should have been fun for me, but it wasn't. I was incapable of feeling pleasure or happiness since my dad left and my mom filed for divorce. I was terrified it would somehow taint me and my friends wouldn't be allowed to hang around with me anymore. I don't know why, but something welled up inside of me and I blurted out, 'My parents are getting a divorce.' Tommy was so nice to me and simply said, 'I'm sorry'—and we went back to the cards and ice cream. I couldn't believe it, he was still my friend! He cared, and it was no big deal to him."

This is how I felt at the time: "A complete and total rush of relief. I finally cleared [it off] my chest, and it didn't kill me or end my friendship. I felt free. I spent years holding this stuff in. I felt free. We went back to what we were doing and *I had fun*. I finally was having fun and not thinking of the divorce anymore."

This is how I feel now as I write it down: "Happiness. It was such a step forward in my life to just be able to live and not feel like I was carrying a huge secret."

Memory Truths

People frequently complain that they have lousy memories. So you just might feel a little pressure when you're instructed to recall something from the past that you would mostly rather forget. Try these techniques to help bring back the truth in your memory:

- *Use visual aids.* Reviewing old photos of you and your family when you were a child can remind you of certain incidents, as well as the feelings associated with them. Even if you need to go to your parents' homes or have photos sent to you, it is worth the effort, because seeing yourself as a child can take you back in a more concrete way.

- *Take a fresh look at yourself.* When you're looking at the photos of yourself, think about how you felt either when the photo was taken or around that time of your life. How do you feel about it now? It's likely that your perspective has changed. You may look at a photo of yourself as a seven-year-old and remember hating your hair because it was curly like Mom's and you wished it was straight like Dad's, who was far away. Now you realize you wanted to identify with him and that's why you felt awful about your hair. You'll probably also realize how cute you were. If you felt homely as a kid, I hope photos will change your mind and allow you to see your cuter, sweeter child self.

- *Be a good observer.* Take time to consider how your family members look in the photos. Are they smiling or serious? How does it feel today to see a photo of your parents together (if you have such a photo)? Do you look different in the photos during the time they were together? Does your attitude seem to change in photos taken during or after the separation? All of these observations are important.

- *Try to recall your school days.* Education represents a huge chunk of your childhood. If you still live near your school, drive by it or even take a walk through the hallways. Trying to remember the names of your teachers from preschool on up is a good way to conjure up memories. Think about who your friends were, what projects you did, and what school events you were involved with. You'll probably be able to associate your school memories with events that were taking place at home during these times. If you don't live near your old school, then find a comfortable place to sit or stand outside your child's school or a local elementary school and start thinking about your school days. You may be surprised to find out what starts coming back to you.

- *Enlist the help of trusted siblings.* Discussing memories with a sibling can help you to remember images and scenes. Of course, your siblings might remember things differently than you do, but if you have a good relationship, you'll learn from their perspectives as well. However, be cautious that the interpretation you explore in your journal is your own and not someone else's. To stay on *your* agenda, ask specific questions about certain memories or events, such as "Do you remember how we were told about the divorce?", "What happened the day after Mom walked out?", or "When do you remember seeing Dad after he remarried?"

- *Turn on some oldies.* Notice how you can remember the lyrics to a song you haven't thought about in twenty, thirty, or even forty years just by hearing the music? Turning on old music is a great way to tune in forgotten memories. When you are thinking and writing about your truth, turn on some of the songs you listened to as a child. This can be your own music or the music your parents played around the house.

- *Wake up your senses.* "Mom smelled like Chanel No. 5, Dad of freshly brewed coffee. Holiday time tasted of gingerbread." Thinking about the smells and tastes of your childhood can re-create the event. Close your eyes and allow your senses to set the scene. Envision what you saw (the room you were in, the clothes you were wearing), what you heard (who did the talking, what tone of voice was used), the smells (was a meal involved, was spring in the air), and so on.

- *Let your kids take you back.* If you have children or grand-children, look at them and consider what was going on in your life when you were their age. What were you thinking in those days? How does it compare to what your kids or grandkids might be thinking about now? Is it similar or very different? How?

A Common Theme

There is rarely such thing as divorce without fighting. Most parents are only deluding themselves if they think they are doing it "in private." The effect on children who are out of sight but not out of hearing distance can be lifelong trouble dealing with conflict. This was the case for Becky.

This is the full memory as best I can recall: "I'm about eight or nine years old and my parents are downstairs screaming and fighting. I'm in my bedroom with my door closed—terrified. My mother stormed out of the house, and at that moment I knew she was never coming back, though she did. I was crying and scared to leave my room. Right after she stormed out, Dad threw open my door, still very angry, and yelled at me, 'What the hell are you crying about?' and slammed my door."

This is how I felt at the time: "Confused that my dad was mad at me, afraid to leave my room, so afraid my mom was gone forever. Desperate."

This is how I feel now as I write it down: "My parents were always fighting, and to this day I never like to get into conflict with people because I don't know how I'll react. I'm afraid I'll end up losing it like my parents and just start yelling. This has actually never happened to me and yet I'm still afraid it will."

Sum Up Your Memories

Summing up is a very important step in this process, and it should be felt, not thought about.

As you're recording your ten memories, you'll experience certain feelings that are similar to those you felt at the time. You're likely to feel sadness, and it could be overwhelming. You might feel angry, resentful, and depressed. There is no shortage of emotions that arise from watching your family get torn apart. Once your memories are committed to paper, go back and review them, then ask yourself this question and write down your response: What do these events and feelings say about my mental map and how I've come to believe who I am?

Next, write a few lines about how you imagine a little child (you) who had these experiences might create a self-image. You can use the following statements to help get you started. Elaborate on each of them:

As a child, was I . . .
Nurtured?
Shown physical demonstrations of love?
Verbally told loving messages?
Told "I love you"? (How often?)
Made to feel protected?
Listened to? (Did my parents "get" me?)
Encouraged to share my voice—my feelings, thoughts, and opinions?
Celebrated?
Happy?
Dealt with honestly?
Taught in a loving manner?

Next, consider the most pivotal child-of-divorce moments in your life and summarize how you felt having to deal with them. Write each one down on a new page in your journal and record your emotional response. Use the following to help:

Finding out about the separation or divorce
Experiencing one parent leaving

Missing the parent who left

Going back and forth between parents

Being a messenger between parents

Hearing negative things about one parent from the other

Being asked to spy on one parent for the other

Having to keep secrets from a parent

Dealing with a parent's new boyfriend or girlfriend

Dealing with a stepparent

Dealing with stepsiblings

How your parents managed school events

How your parents celebrated your birthday

Learning about child support

Worrying about family finances

Discovering or being told that one parent was unfaithful

················· MEMORIES ·················
Being the Fifth Wheel

Each one of us, especially as a child, wants to feel normal. Divorce automatically makes a child feel like he or she is from a "broken" family and that everyone else is from a normal one. It bleeds into every part of our lives, and soon everything about us feels abnormal, as in this memory from Bradley.

This is the full memory as best I can recall: "While at Disneyland with my aunt and her family, I remember having so much fun, but it was mixed with a sense of bitterness."

This is how I felt at the time: "I felt like the fifth wheel. My beautiful aunt was there with her beautiful family, and they allowed me to come along. I remember seeing the babies in a stroller and thinking how easy their life was to have a mom and dad who loved them. Theirs was a 'normal' family, and I no longer had that. I remember taking a picture with them and thinking how ugly I must have looked next to them."

This is how I feel now as I write it down: "When I look at the picture now, I know I wasn't ugly, but I consistently wore a headband to cover my forehead because I thought it was huge. I even thought they were lucky to not have huge foreheads like mine. I was desperately trying to change the image of how I saw myself. I tried to make myself look better by covering what I perceived to be my flaws instead of accepting or loving myself as I was. I may have succeeded in covering my 'flaw,' but I have to admit now that I looked a bit ridiculous in the process. I guess I had low self-worth."

How Truth Unfolds

Finding the truth can be a taxing process, and you will most likely find yourself quite spent by the end of the week. Make sure to congratulate yourself and remind yourself that this is an important and necessary step in achieving your desire for change. By the end of the week, you will probably have proven to yourself that having been a child of divorce has had much more of an effect on your life than you ever realized.

Before you begin, it will be helpful to see an in-depth example of how this process unfolds. Below you will find journal entries graciously shared by Sarah from my research group. As you will see, Sarah has a lot of feelings that are still very raw and fresh after more than twenty years. Not only did she lose her sense of family, she also felt completely lost because of her mother's exit from her daily life. Things continued to spiral, leaving her in an unprotected position.

Sarah and Her Truth Journal

Sarah is a thirty-two-year-old physical therapist. She has had a few—she'd say too many—failed relationships. When she started the program, one of her major obstacles to happiness was her distrust of men. When she meets a guy whose company she really enjoys and the feeling is mutual, she gets such feelings of fear and dread that he's going to drop her that it becomes a self-fulfilling prophecy. The man eventually moves on because he senses that she doesn't trust him.

Sarah wants true love and desperately wants to have children, but she's plagued with doubt that it ever will happen. At times she questions if she is even fit to be a mother, because she's not sure how to do the job. Her mother is the one who broke up the family and moved out when Sarah was only ten.

The "Sarah's Memory" sections that follow are all verbatim excerpts from Sarah's journal.

Sarah's Memory: The Announcement of the Divorce

This is the full memory as best I can recall: I'm ten. It's January and probably within one to three weeks after Christmas when my parents told us they were getting a divorce. The fact that I can't remember the exact date bugs me, because I'm the one people go to when they want details. Yet this memory is sort of blurry, sort of like when you do a chalk drawing on the sidewalk and then rub your hands all over it. My feeling about the timing of the announcement is that my parents wanted to spare [us sadness at] Christmas. (I would rather they had just spared [me for] the rest of my life and not just one holiday.)

It was a Saturday morning, the day the whole family always had breakfast together. Until then everything had been perfect, or so it seemed. I had two parents who never fought. Everyone was always in my backyard, riding bikes, climbing trees, or going to the park. I have one picture in my drawer of my family before the divorce that reminds me of a time when everything was fine. I don't like to just stumble upon it because it brings back such mixed emotions about it all. It reminds me of a time when everything was fine—better than fine.

On this Saturday morning we were eating something like waffles or pancakes, because I remember the syrup. We were all sitting around the table, probably in our pajamas. I had finished eating, and the dishes were still on the table. Nothing seemed out of the ordinary, other than some general uneasiness I'd had since dinner last night. No one was fighting. Everything was otherwise normal and fine. And then being normal and fine ended. I don't remember who exactly said what. I know we were told that they had something to tell us. Essentially they said they were going to have a "trial separation" and that my mom was going to move out.

Nothing was ever the same again. My mom would be moving to the city (we lived in the suburbs), and we would still see her but be staying in the house with my dad. I remember staring at the syrup swirls on my plate. I know I did not say a word.

This is how I felt at the time: Totally shocked and stunned. I couldn't believe this was happening. Everything was *fine*! I had never once heard my parents fight or say a mean word to each other (this was about to change, little did I grasp at the time). How did my perfect life just fall apart in an instant without any real warning? I'm pretty sure this was the day I first felt numb, because I'm sure I had to feel sad. But I don't remember it. I more remember being almost panicked and terrified. They wanted me to live *without my mom?* I also remember not wanting anyone else to know, so I must have felt some element of shame. If I could have kept it a secret from everyone else in my life, I would have.

This is how I feel now as I write it down: As I sit here, the whole "trial" thing makes me angry. I know they were probably trying to be nice and lessen the blow—and maybe they really did think it was a trial separation. I think maybe my dad thought it was a trial also, but I'd be willing to bet my mom knew it was permanent from the start. Either way, I feel like I was lied to and tricked. Oh, and stabbed in the back.

Sarah's Memory: Feeling Abandoned As Mom Moves Out

This is the full memory as best I can recall: I don't remember my mom moving out at all. I just remember her apartment in the city and visiting it for the first time. It was so strange because there was furniture from our house there, and it seemed both familiar and out of place in this new apartment all at the same time. There was a back porch, and I would like to sit out back if the weather was nice. It looked out onto the yards of the two homes next door. I remember one family having a big party one night and me just sitting outside watching them enjoy themselves all together. That seemed more normal to me than being inside the apartment, because it just reminded me that nothing was normal anymore.

This is how I felt at the time: I felt like an outsider in my mom's life, alone, wanting everything to go back to how it was before, waiting for this "trial" to be over.

This is how I feel now as I write it down: Sad and lonely.

Sarah's Memory: Caught in the Middle

This is the full memory as best I can recall: The first fight. I will never forget this. I was now eleven, and it was three months after my mom moved out. My parents had never fought, at least not in front of me, and they weren't often alone without us at least in the house, so I'm pretty sure they never fought. The first fight was over the phone.

I was at home with my dad, and I don't know who called whom. All I know is that my dad put me on the phone with my mom so that I could say hi. This is one of those chalk-drawing memories—parts have been smudged out. What ended up happening was that they started fighting with each other, but through me. They didn't get on the phone to yell at each other, I had to act as the intermediary. How long did the fight last? I have no real idea. In my mind it was an eternity. My dad would tell me something horrible and hurtful to say to my mom, and she'd try to top it. Only, every insult and harsh word they threw at each other felt like it was directed at me. And then I had to say it out loud, and I wanted to disappear.

I'm not even sure why they needed me, because by that point they were both yelling and screaming so loud I'm sure I wasn't needed as a message conveyor. But the worst part was when my mom had me "tell" my dad that she should never have married him, that it was the worst mistake she had ever made in her whole life, that she should have left years ago, and that there wasn't anything good about being married to him. That wasn't the life she wanted ever again.

I have no idea if that was the end of the fight. I literally don't remember. I don't have any idea how the fight ended. Did I just walk away? Did my dad finally take the phone and hang it up? Did I say goodbye? No idea. But I do remember feeling at that moment that my mom was never going to come home. That no matter how long I waited, she was not going to come home. It wasn't really a "trial." It was going to be forever. That was also when I realized that she felt the marriage was a mistake and that there wasn't anything good about it—just like she said. So if the marriage was a mistake, and I was something that came out of this marriage, then I also must be a mistake, because she just said that nothing good came out of it.

Until that point I think I thought that maybe while she was away, she would miss me enough and realize what a mistake she had made and come back—if only to get me. Maybe that alone might fix the situation. Her loving my dad was kind of second-ary—I just wanted to be sure she loved *me*. Then maybe my family might have a chance of getting back together, especially since it was a trial separation. Only, now that theory was blown, because not only was I not worth coming back for, I was now a horrible mistake. All those things made her leave, and she wasn't ever going to come back home.

This is how I felt at the time: Unloved, unlovable, unworthy, alone, like a failure. I'm sure I was sad, even though I didn't cry (then or ever). I didn't really think that it was exactly my fault that my mom left, but I felt very strongly that there was clearly something so wrong or flawed with me that it wasn't worth it to her to stay or to bring me with her.

This is how I feel now as I write it down: I feel pretty much the same now, only with a lot of numbness mixed in. I've run through this memory a million times and have never written it down. It's the same conversation with myself over and over and over again. It always ends with me being worthless, unlovable, and funda-mentally flawed. It's like if someone could just tell me what was so wrong with me, I'd do whatever I need to do to fix it. Only, I really wonder if it's fixable, and I figure it's so fundamental that I'm just forever defective.

I still can't figure out how in the short time right after the divorce, only about four months, I went from so happy and feel-ing loved and loving my life to feeling like I was destroyed and that everything had gone horribly wrong.

Sarah's Memory: He Shrank My Sweater!

This is the full memory as best I can recall: My dad shrank my favorite sweater. Seems like a ridiculous memory, but it totally sticks out in my mind. Essentially, it happened not too long after my mom left. My dad was doing laundry and washed my sweater in hot water and put it in the dryer. It literally shrank to such a small size that I ended up giving it to my four-year-old cousin. I remember my dad holding it up and apologizing for ruining it.

This is how I felt at the time: Like, seriously, I was left behind with a guy who can't even wash a sweater? How could anyone think that was a good idea? That was the beginning of the realization that I better learn to take care of myself. If he couldn't wash a sweater, what else was he going to mess up?

This is how I feel now as I write it down: I am actually still somewhat ticked—it was my favorite sweater—but I'm more incredulous that a grown woman had left her preteen daughter to be primarily raised by a guy when I was going to have lots of girl growing-up issues that no girl ever, ever, ever wants to address with her dad. I don't care how great a dad you are, girl issues and dads just don't mix! Even if discussing that stuff was not uncomfortable (which it surely was), he had no idea what any of it was like—nor could he ever. As a girl in that situation, you kind of feel lost, without direction, and alone, because there's no one around who really has a true clue what all this girl maturing stuff is like.

This is how I feel now as I write it down: So maybe this memory was more about feeling abandoned and not as much about the sweater.

Sarah's Memory: Abandoned—Twice

This is the full memory as best I can recall: When my dad decided to start dating, I had a little bit of a hard time with this, even though my mom had already started dating (but nothing serious). While I wasn't too thrilled with him at this point, at least he hadn't been the one to abandon me. He started dating about seven months after my mom left, and I was a little shocked. I guess I thought he should be working harder to try to get my mom back instead of dating other people. I wasn't even used to the idea that they were apart, and every day was still a struggle.

That said, the first person he dated I actually kind of liked. She was really nice; she had two daughters, and we got along quite well. It only lasted a couple of months and then she was gone.

Within a couple of months after that my dad met someone at church. Her name was Lori, and I hated her immediately. She was not particularly warm or nice. Nice enough if your dad wasn't dating her, I suppose. She also had a daughter (Melanie) who was five years old. I was eleven at the time and felt she was a brat. Pretty much, I think Lori just had a strong personality and an attitude that it was her way or the highway.

My brother and I became sort of second-class citizens at this point. My dad was happy to go along with whatever she said, and I was wishing he'd take the highway! I thought if I waited that this would end like the other one did. But it didn't, and my dad ended up marrying her.

Lori was the driving force behind many of his decisions, and she was quick to insult and belittle my mom to me every chance she got. Not that she had even met my mom at this point, but she was sure to tell me what a horrible person she was. The only time I ever said something back was once when I whispered, "But you don't know her." Her response to me was "No, I know you."

This is how I felt at the time: Once I realized that my dad seemed more vested in this new woman than in his children, it was like he had abandoned me also. I felt so horrible and attacked when Lori would attack my mom. I was so alone. The world really was unsafe at this point. I really felt like no one loved me, and I had no idea what was so wrong with me that I couldn't keep this from happening.

This is how I feel now as I write it down: When I look back at that situation, I really feel that my dad started dating too soon. However, I don't know when the right time is (even if you're dating a nice person). Just that seven months afterward is too soon.

Sarah's Memory: It Was Like Living in Jail

This is the full memory as best I can recall: My brother moves out. I'm sixteen and my brother is not quite fourteen. My brother was always in trouble from the minute he was born. And I was a goody-goody who really tried not to do anything wrong. My dad seemed to like me. He never seemed to like my brother. And my stepmother (or stepmonster, as I called her) hated him.

When they were getting ready to get married, something had to give. And essentially my brother was sent to live with my mom—which I wanted so much! But it wasn't me who was going. It would seem like maybe I could have said something, but that wasn't possible. How could I possibly do that to my dad? How could I just abandon him? Would that make him hate me as much as he hated my mom? But it was more than that. Mom actually moved back to the suburb where we had lived so my brother could live with her. Not *me*, but my brother, who had always been in trouble his whole life. It was like a slap in the face. I was the one who never made trouble, did well in school, and appeared to be totally fine. Why did he get rewarded for his bad behavior? So I also couldn't say anything because I was scared my mom would say she didn't want me—only him. It was damned if I did and damned if I didn't. Instead I just got to stay in a house where I felt totally lonely and disliked by over half the people in the house. It was like living in jail.

This is how I felt at the time: Scared to say what I really wanted, and scared that if I did, I would get an answer that would crush me more. Scared that my dad would hate me if I did say what I really wanted. I was alone. Totally jealous of my brother. I felt like there was no way out of the situation. I also didn't get why my mom moved back to the suburbs for him, but not for us both. I felt like I was drowning. Not only did I have to live with my dad and only see my mom every two weeks, but now the wicked witch and her little brat were moving into my house. It was like I was lost in my own home. And it solidified my feelings of aloneness.

This is how I feel now as I write it down: I have a hard time with the idea of kids giving input into custody because of this. First of all, wouldn't the world feel like a safer place if adults made good and fair decisions? The pressure to say you want to live with a parent or don't want to live with a parent is crushing. So in a way it seems less stressful to just take the kids out of the equation and not give them that pressure and fear of hurting someone. But then again, can you get what you want if you don't say it? I don't know the answer to this.

Sarah's Memory: Holidays Were the Worst

This is the full memory as best I can recall: Holidays. They were all pretty much the same, didn't matter which holiday it was. It always consisted of having to go to one house, eat a meal, then go to another house and eat another meal. Eating two Thanksgiving dinners is not fun. And really, I just wanted to go with my mom's family. I have a lot of cousins, and we all get along really well. Plus my mom's family is really funny (and sarcastic), and there's generally going to be laughter when you're there. Add to that, I saw my dad all the time, and any time away from my stepmonster was a good thing. But I still had to do both. I just remember how I started to dread holidays. And of course there would be disagreements about when we would be where and with whom.

This is how I felt at the time: Holidays always made me feel caught in the middle, like my enjoyment of them was sacrificed so that each parent could have his or her fair share. And eating two meals was physically uncomfortable.

This is how I feel now as I write it down: Thinking that ten memories are not enough. If I sat here long enough, I could probably keep going with more.

Sarah's Memory: Transition Anxiety

This is the full memory as best I can recall: Transitions between parents. When I was young, transitions were not fun, especially as I usually had to take some bus or train and would get motion sickness. But it did almost provide some sort of decompression time between parents, because you really do have to almost switch to a different mode, depending on which parent you're with. It's like you can't exactly be just you, you also have to be who they want you to be. Anyway, I hated the transitions, but I always just figured it was what it was.

Then I got to be about twenty-three years old. I was in physical therapy school near home but not living at home. I started to have a really bad time leaving either parent's house. It didn't matter which parent it was or where I was going. Just the act of leaving made me feel horrible. I would sit in the car and just literally shake for about ten minutes. At my dad's I'd usually have to leave the driveway, and I'd go to the park down the street and sit there because I didn't want them wondering what I was doing just sitting in the car. After about ten minutes it would get better, but I never really figured out what it was. It took a number of years for it to go away.

This is how I felt at the time: I'm not even sure. I just knew that I hurt a lot when I would leave. I didn't ever really figure out why. I mean, I could come and go of my own free will at that point. I could pretty much see whichever parent I wanted when I wanted. It didn't, and still doesn't, make any sense to me why leaving would affect me so much at that point. Once it went away after a few years, I didn't really think of it again until now. It probably meant something, I just have no idea what.

This is how I feel now as I write it down: Remembering the transitions as a child reminds me of the frustration I felt and how sad I was to have to do it. Why couldn't they have just gotten along and been together?

Sarah's Memory: A Painful yet Sacred Reminder

This is the full memory as best I can recall: I have one picture of my whole family (mom, dad, brother, and me) that was taken when I was younger (around six years old) at my aunt and uncle's wedding. It would definitely fall into the idea of this memory when everything was great and secure and amazing. I know exactly where this picture is in my desk drawer, because I can only look at it when I want to look at it. I do not like to stumble upon it without meaning to. The picture reminds me of the time when everything *was* fine—*better* than fine. It reminds me that there was once this family that seemed to be everything I could have ever wanted. There was love and security. That picture is almost like a dream. Like I almost wonder if that part of my life really happened. It makes me want something that was so great but that I can never have back again. So it's a double-edged sword. It brings up reminders of much better times but also that those times are gone. What I wouldn't give to be able to have that back for even just a little while.

This is how I felt at the time: At the time the picture was taken, I felt secure. I felt loved and like everything was fine.

This is how I feel now as I write it down: If I look at that picture now, it just makes me wish that I could climb out of my life now and into that picture.

Sarah's Memory: A Shameful Secret

This is the full memory as best I can recall: I don't want to even write this memory. I'd like to never think of it again, but leaving it out is like a lie. A really big lie. And it seems like it's not really divorce related, but it is in a sideways sort of way. I feel the need to do some background information: I lived next door to my best friend's family. They had a mom, dad, and seven kids. One of their daughters, Jessica, and I had been friends since we were practically infants. I fit right into the "big family" dynamic, and it became like a second home for me.

Jessica had a brother, John, who was four years older than us, and two younger brothers. Her brothers felt as much like brothers to me as my own brother did. I was so much a part of their family that Jes's parents would even call me their daughter. Now, that doesn't mean that I told them anything about how I was feeling about what was going on in my own house. The fact that my own parents stabbed me in the back and betrayed me with the divorce meant that all adults weren't safe.

My dad had to find someone to watch us five days a week after school, since he didn't come home until late in the afternoon. He ended up hiring John, Jessica's older brother. We were eleven, so John was fifteen. Plus his mom was home right next door, so it seemed like a good situation and a safe situation. And it was. At first.

John started watching us when school started in August. Everything was fine. He wasn't the most fun babysitter, but then again, it was like having your brother watch you.

Cut to Christmas. It was after Christmas, and the tree was still up. It was during winter vacation and so John was watching us during the day while my dad was at work. My brother was downstairs in the basement playing video games with John's younger brother, and I had gone over to lie under the Christmas tree and look up at the lights. Lying under the Christmas tree was one of my favorite things to do because I used to think the colored lights were so pretty, and if you lie under the tree and look up, you see this sea of beautiful lights. And they were pretty—until John decided to lie down next to me. Only he wasn't interested in looking at Christmas lights.

I can't figure out a way to write this that doesn't make me feel sick, and I'm not interested in providing details. I don't think they really matter. Let's just say that John was more interested in touching me in places that he should not. I just remember being frozen and willing this not to happen. I remember saying I didn't like it. He said that he was going to keep going until he taught me to like it. So I lied and said I liked it, thinking he would then stop. He then said that since I now liked it, he wanted to give me what I liked.

Almost every day was like that. It didn't matter where I was in my house, I wasn't safe. He'd pop locks on doors. Sometimes it was only fifteen minutes, other times (especially if it was a day off of school) it could be an hour or two. The only reason I knew the time was that I'd look at the clock or my watch when it started and when it ended. Other than that, I pretty much checked out. I wasn't numb—I was gone. I don't exactly know where my mind went, but it went away. I don't remember thinking anything specific, just this blankness. Almost like an absence of thought. It's a very surreal experience. I'd usually snap back to reality toward the end because it would always end when I'd have to tell him that I liked what he was doing. Then I'd have to tell him what I liked best. Then I'd have to thank him for making me feel so good. That might have actually been worse than the actual physical stuff.

But the worst day was when it was going on and I looked over and saw my brother watching. I was fairly exposed at this point and would not have wanted him to see any of what was exposed under normal circumstances, but it was even worse with what he got to see happening. My brother was nine years old at the time, and he just stood there and stared until John told him to walk away; he seemed to be in shock.

This went on for a number of months. I would try to not be home, but eventually I'd have to be home. I needed to find a way to make it stop. Since I wasn't sure about how my parents would handle this, I stayed silent. I was scared they wouldn't believe me or care.

Why I ultimately decided I could not tell: I didn't know what was going to happen once I told. I had no control over that, and I did not trust the adults in my life to make good decisions, or at least the decisions I wanted. I played through the options in my head. The best was that John would not be allowed to babysit and that it would be over. But then, would I still be allowed to be friends with Jessica? Was I going to lose my other family? Those were not options I could live with. And I could not control if those things happened or not. So telling was not an option. I would rather have had Jessica and that family than to lose them. Oh, and then there was the fact that I was scared to death and so ashamed.

How I made it stop: It took me a little time, but I devised a plan. What I needed was John out of my house. I needed a new babysitter. How did I do that? No idea exactly, but that was only going to happen if John was unable to babysit anymore. Since he wasn't going to quit, I had to get him "fired" in some way. So one day I was at Jessica's house. We were baking cookies with her mom. As we cracked eggs and stirred in flour, I complained about my brother (normal sister stuff). Then I worked in how at least my brother would play video games for hours with John (which was true), so at least they would leave me alone. Video games were a big no-no in John's house. Jes, always one to get her brother in trouble, even chimed in how all he did at my house was play video games. This made their mom angry (that was my hope—my only hope). She said something to the effect that that wasn't appropriate when you were babysitting because you weren't paid to play video games. We agreed, and it was dropped for the time being, but I knew John was going to get in trouble. Sure enough, John's parents made him give my dad two weeks notice and he had to "'fess up" about the video games to my dad as the reason. John wasn't happy, but at least it was only two more weeks of hell. And then I went to someone else's house to get babysat, and I was free.

This is how I felt at the time: While it was going on, I literally felt nothing. All the rest of the time I felt sick, horribly ashamed, and dirty. And angry toward my parents. I actually blamed my parents for a big part of it. They were the ones who left me alone to care for myself. If they hadn't split up, I'd still be watched by the family down the street, and this would never have happened. I felt like it was partly their fault that I was being tortured in this way in my own house. That they could not save me (not really fair, since they had no idea what was going on, but, hell, it wasn't fair that it was happening). And if I had any shred of self-worth left by the time it started (which wouldn't have been much, anyway) that was pretty much gone.

This is how I feel now as I write it down: Well, I felt sick while writing this down. As an adult, I shockingly still feel like my parents are to blame, although logically I know it's not true. Especially since my brother tried to tell my mom, and I made him stop. It's like had they been doing their job and not left me alone, this would never have happened. I'm a little proud of myself that I was able to make it stop—even though it was a crapshoot and I got really lucky that it went how I hoped. I also logically know that no child is ever to blame for that happening to them, but I still feel ashamed as well. Like maybe if I had been brave enough to fight back instead of being frozen, it might not have happened. I didn't really want anyone to ever know (which is why I didn't want to write this memory down). And it still feeds into the general feeling that I'm deserving of these bad things that happened to me. Who says numb isn't better?

Sarah's Present Feelings about Her Past

"What do these events and feelings say about my mental map and who I've become?" Sarah continues in her journal. "I have a great deal of feelings and memories that I have tried to swallow in some way. Obviously, as I look at them, I can see how they would cause me to have failed relationships and have huge issues with trust. I just can't hide from them anymore. I must find a way to live with them and find some way to get over them somehow. Even though I have tried to not think about these things, when you add them up they really are me now. I wanted them to go away, but they're still following me. I still feel horrible, like I'm just this insignificant person walking around who isn't worth anything. Like I can't get anything right. Just knowing that the world is not a safe place and that no matter what I do, I never feel like I've found a safe place because I can't trust people to not hurt me. If my own parents could make me feel like this, I can't take a chance with other people. I can't ever put my guard down, even around myself, because even my own feelings feel like they could destroy me at any minute if I dared to really experience them."

The following list shows Sarah's responses to the nurturance requirements we listed earlier.

As a child, was I . . .

Nurtured? "Before the split I was nurtured, yes. After the split I didn't feel it at all."

Shown physical demonstrations of love? "Before the split, yes. Lots of snuggling while watching a favorite show or reading a book. After the divorce, it turned more cursory and there was no warm feeling attached to it."

Verbally told loving messages? "Before the divorce, somewhat; after, not so much. My parents weren't big verbal expressers of feelings."

Told "I love you" (how often)? "Before the split, I was told 'I love you' at the very least when I left for school in the morning and when I went to bed every night. After, it seemed like that almost stopped entirely."

Made to feel protected? "Before the divorce, I felt very protected, but after, not only did I feel unprotected but my parents were the ones who were doing the attacking."

Listened to? "Before the divorce, I felt that my parents seemed to understand me and listened to what I had to say. Afterward, I pretty much stopped speaking about anything, but I don't think they would have 'got' me or understood even if I had spoken up."

Encouraged to share my voice? "Before, I was sort of encouraged to share my voice. My family was more of a 'do what you're told when you're told to do it' kind of household. When they said jump, it was my job to say, 'How high?' My dad was more strict than my mom, so she did kind of soften that a bit, but after the divorce, she left, and then it felt like dictatorial rule. No sharing going on there."

Celebrated? "Before, yes; afterward, it felt more like I was managed."

Happy? "Before the divorce, I was happy! After, no."

Dealt with honestly? "Well, the whole thing with the 'trial separation' was pretty much a lie. However, most of the time I wasn't even dealt with at all."

Taught in a loving manner? "Before, yes; after, I felt more like I had to fend for myself. No one taught me or guided me after the divorce."

Sarah added this note:

When I considered the items on this list, it felt like most of them were present before the split. No wonder I felt like my life was perfect. And the fact that those aspects of parenting seemed to disappear once my parents divorced—no wonder I felt so crappy.

This is how Sarah responded to her most pivotal child-of-divorce moments:

Finding out about the separation or divorce: "Shocked, stunned, scared, sad, angry."

Experiencing one parent leaving: "Alone, sad, like I wasn't worth staying for."

Missing the parent who left: "Sad and desperate."

Going back and forth between parents: "Going back and forth between parents was particularly hurtful. I felt like an inconvenience and unimportant to them because neither would drive us. It made me feel like I wasn't even worth the time and energy."

Being a messenger between parents: "It made me angry that they had to make their problem with communication my problem. They made it seem like their arguing was more important than sparing me the terrible feelings it caused me."

Hearing negative things about one parent from the other: "Hearing negative things about one parent from the other is like having those things said directly to yourself. After hearing them enough, you then begin to believe that they really are about you, too."

Dealing with a parent's new boyfriend or girlfriend; dealing with a stepparent: "It made me very angry and feel even more worthless when my dad's new significant other treated me like an insignificant piece of dirt and pretended she was in charge of me over my real parent. The worst part about the experience was when my dad would not stand up to protect me."

Dealing with stepsiblings: "More of an annoyance. We coexisted in the same house without much meaningful interaction."

How your parents managed school events: "My parents usually managed to hold it together in public if they were both there, but it would still make me somewhat anxious. Depending on my age, there were certain things that one or neither of them would even show up for. This actually started to be my preferred option."

How your parents celebrated your birthday: "Birthdays just kind of sucked all around. They became more like a reminder of the 'big mistake' my mom had made."

Learning about child support: "These conversations or arguments made me feel unsafe. It made me feel like these adults couldn't even handle that, so how could they care for me? I was also conflicted about the topic because I couldn't figure out 'who was right.'"

Worrying about family finances: "This caused terrible stress for me."

Discovering or being told that one parent was unfaithful: (Not applicable in this case.)

Get Ready to Write

Now it's your turn. Sarah's step 2 journal writing should give you a sense of how to start getting your mental map down on paper. Try to be as specific as possible as you recall events and feelings. Don't limit yourself. Write as though you were telling it to someone. No editing! When you are done, you will be amazed what it feels like to see all of those memories down on paper in one place.

Take it all in and get ready for step 3.

5

Reflect Clearly
on the Past

Step 3, Week 3

You've had many things go wrong in your life. Most likely you've faced one disappointment after another. It's not as though you didn't try or that you don't continue to try. Maybe you try *really hard* and things still do not go the way you planned. You've really never been able to understand why it all happens and why it always happens to you.

But now you're beginning to figure it out. Step 3 will bring you the clarity you need to change. You've traced your mental map and have seen your life on autopilot. Is it any wonder that this has led you to so many unhappy situations and experiences? But your life is more in focus now, because your past is in focus. You now know the truth, *your* truth. Even if it still feels a bit uncomfortable, keep in mind that recalling memories is just a small bump in the road leading to changing the course of your autopilot.

Brace yourself, though; the road just might get a bit rocky this week, because you're going to take a fresh look at pivotal moments in your life from childhood through adulthood. This time, and probably for the first time, you're going to look at them through the lens of the truth.

There might be painful moments as you begin to realize that parts of your past didn't have to turn out the way they did. If only you had been on a different autopilot, you could have had a different life. I encourage you to do your best not to let this thought get you down. In the end, this week will be uplifting. It will give you incredible inspiration and serve as your guide to achieve a whole new life in which you are finally in control. You'll see your life in a whole new light. But before we go there, I want to help you understand why it has been so difficult for you to overturn the mindset that has kept you living in the emotional world of your childhood.

Flashbacks in the Brain

How many times have you said to yourself, "I should have known better" or "I can't believe I acted that way" or "I fell for the wrong person—again." It's your autopilot, the way your brain has trained you to respond and react. You say you have bad habits? It's your brain on autopilot again.

You have instinctive ways of behaving and acting in certain situations because of the way your brain is programmed and tied to your past; this is the autopilot of your life. Although you are unaware of it, your brain has been programmed to respond today the way it did under similar circumstances in your past, even when you consciously try to do the opposite. In short, it is your mindset.

Your mindset keeps you tied to your past, and you demonstrate this time and again through your behavior and emotions.

If you come home at the end of the day cursing yourself for doing something or acting in a way that was not your intention, you can learn to say that this isn't the real you. You can now understand that your "child mind" made you do it. There are three mechanisms by which your brain manipulates your behavior:

1. Familiarity
2. Proving your childhood right
3. Control

These are your mental enemies. Before you undertake this week's exercises, you need to get to know these mechanisms so you can understand the way they work against you. The only way you'll ever to able to break the hold they have on you is to be able to recognize when they are advancing.

A Physical Response to Childhood

Here is a simple example of how powerful childhood experiences can be: At age six you were attacked by a German shepherd that bit your leg while you were riding your bicycle. How do you think you might react at age sixty if a Yorkie came charging at your leg? Your blood pressure and pulse rate would zoom, and you could win a medal for how high you jumped.

What we learn about the world as children affects our physiology. Not only do we react emotionally to certain situations, but our bodies support the reaction as well.

For example, if you were screamed at a great deal as a child, your heart might begin racing much faster than someone else's when you hear yelling as an adult. If your mother or your father was cold and not physically demonstrative, your body might tense up when your spouse wants to just sit and wrap you in his or her arms for a while. If your father humiliated you when you were a kid, your blood pressure might rise more than usual when your boss criticizes your work.

This demonstrates the extreme fine-tuning of your mental map. It affects you emotionally *and* physically.

Manage the Damage: Familiarity

The need to manage the damage of familiarity is the most counterintuitive concept you'll read about in this book. Most people expect that someone who experiences a painful event in childhood will go out of his or her way to avoid ever repeating it in adulthood. For example, if you had parents who fought all of the time and never hugged you or said they loved you, you swear that you'll marry someone who is tender and loving and that the two of you will never fight. If you wore hand-me-downs as a kid because Dad rarely came through with child support, you swear you'll work hard so your kids never have to go hungry and underdressed. If you felt starved for affection because your parents weren't particularly snuggly, you know you'll give your kids the kind of love you didn't get.

This is true—sometimes. It does happen, but only for a minority of people. Most people end up right back where they started. If you're a child of divorce, you have a greater chance of ending up in a troubled marriage, even though you vowed never to end up like your parents. If you lived hand-to-mouth as a child, there is a good chance you'll have trouble managing money as an adult.

Seems odd, doesn't it? It almost doesn't make sense that we'd allow ourselves to fall into the same trap. Why would you willingly enter a marriage that was doomed from the start? Why would you willingly gamble your money away and risk your family's security? Why would you willingly be cold and distant with your children?

In short, it's because that's the way you learned to act as a child. It's what's familiar to you. Your mental map is always ready to lead you to familiar ground. Your autopilot is stronger than your will. As much as you'd like life to be different, your mental map will take you down the path of familiarity if you let it. And you do let it, because you don't realize it's happening in the first place.

Think of it like learning how to talk. If you grew up speaking French, imagine how difficult it would be to suddenly have to switch to English as an adult. You'd have to concentrate on every word—a real effort. If you've ever been forced to communicate in a foreign language, think of how easy it is to slip back into your native language—and how natural it feels.

The way you respond to adult experiences is very similar. Your mental map keeps taking you back to the same trails you blazed as a kid. New experiences produce the same old results. You'll yell at your spouse or kids when you don't mean to. You'll make a sarcastic comment that ticks off the boss. You'll compulsively eat when things don't go your way. These responses come naturally because they feel so familiar.

Familiarity is your enemy. It keeps sucking you in and pretending to make perfect sense in the moment. Your mind convinces you that your mental map is right on course. There's no other way to explain it. After all, no one ever says, "I know my parents' marriage was a mess, and I'm comfortable being in the same circumstances. So let me pass up this lover who's really nice and caring and go find myself a real good challenge."

Instead, you invent sound reasoning to get you to the same old place. I can't tell you how many times I've heard women say, "He's so nice, cuddly, kind—just too much." Huh? What did I miss? Too much "nice"? You can convince yourself of anything, even that "too kind" implies weakness and is unattractive.

You do this because of the way it makes you feel.

....

JESSICA'S STORY
It "Feels" Familiar

The mind is clever in its deception. It catches you unguarded in situations that only appear to be different from your childhood. Why does a woman who had an unloving father who treated her poorly marry a man who is emotionally detached and has a bad temper? Why would a man who was abandoned as a child marry a woman who is already twice divorced and claims that everything was always her husband's fault? The mind is drawing you into a situation in which you will experience the *same feelings* that you felt as a child. More often, however, it happens in ways that are not always obvious.

A perfect example is a woman who went through this program whom I'll call Jessica. Jessica had a father who never said "I love you," who could barely could stand to be around her, and who saw her only a handful of times after her parents divorced. Jessica didn't marry a man just like her father; her husband was quite the opposite. Through the program, however, she realized that her past provoked her to have the same feelings of abandonment in her marriage.

Jessica started out in her marriage thinking she was so lucky. She had married a very loving man—touchy-feely, thoughtful, and kind. He was not at all like her dad. Joe was an entrepreneur and quite successful. He traveled a lot. No problem—Jessica traveled with him, and he was thrilled.

Then their first baby arrived, and Jessica could no longer accompany her husband on business trips. She missed him a lot. She often complained and brooded about him being away so often. He called frequently and tried to keep his trips short, but as his business grew, so did his time away from home. Jessica felt isolated, alone, and abandoned by her husband, just as she had felt abandoned by her father. She resented Joe, just as she had resented her dad.

Jessica didn't marry a man just like her father, but she married a man who made her *feel* the way her dad made her feel: insignificant. She pictured herself right back where she had started as a little girl, feeling out of control and lost and, ironically, caring for a baby all by herself, just as she had cared for her little sister when her parents split up.

Breaking the habit of familiarity isn't easy. It takes you out of your comfort zone. This is what we all do with our mental maps. When push comes to shove and the larger life issues present themselves, we fall back into old patterns that have been ingrained. This is exactly what happened to Jessica.

Manage the Damage: Proving Your Childhood Right

It seems so logical: If you had a parent who was mean, you'll seek a spouse who is nice. If you felt lost and ungrounded as a child, you'll want to find a supportive community and belong to its local organizations as an adult. If you lived hand-to-mouth as a child, you'll try to get a good job and save your money as an adult.

It doesn't happen this way, however, and this is one of the most perplexing reflexes to comprehend.

Imagine that a little girl wants desperately to be loved and nurtured but that this doesn't happen in a healthy way. As a result, she is led to believe something different about herself. She believes she is undesirable to her parents and grows up to be an adult who, believe it or not, still desires her parents' approval and love. As a grown-up, she is still in a mental tussle with her parents to prove her value. She accomplishes this by getting her parents' approval through the approval of another adult—often a lover or a spouse, in this type of circumstance. She wants to feel her *parents'* approval, and in order to do that, she must reinvent as closely as possible the same mental scenario of her childhood. She must work hard at getting her husband's love and approval because she had to work hard at getting her parents' love and approval (even though she often didn't get it).

So what kind of husband is she going to end up with? Not a loving, caring man. He would be no challenge at all because he's so giving and approving. He doesn't remind her of her parents at all. Instead, she needs a man who wants to make her work to get his approval. He does not dole out genuine approval freely. When he does give his approval, the little girl inside the woman gets an emotional lift, as though to say, "I've won!" But that little lift can never fill the deep void from childhood.

Also, in due course, this kind of man will soon find something about her to complain about or to use as an excuse to emotionally distance himself from her. This will cause her to rise up to the challenge of approval all over again. If, by some chance, he becomes a more approving man, she still will be uncomfortable with it and will need to find a way back to the struggle for acceptance.

Next she ratchets up the challenge. She'll even do things to make him disapprove, just to reset the scene and get her back to the same feelings she had as a little girl struggling to get love and affection.

Getting approval feels good only when it comes from a person who, in her mind, represents someone like her parents. It's a vicious cycle that continues indefinitely until you learn how to put a stop to it.

STACY'S STORY
Pushing Loved Ones Away

Stacy went through the program and candidly shared that it angered her to learn that her mindset was drawing her back to the emotions she dealt with in childhood. She discovered that she had a history of relationships, both romantic and otherwise, in which people were inconsiderate and acted inappropriately. She realized that she kept repeating the same mistakes because she made excuses for these people. She had convinced herself that she wasn't "needy"—by which she meant that she didn't need people who were thoughtful. She rationalized her need for independence because of what she went through when her parents divorced. She used this sense of independence as a way to keep herself in her familiar zone of people not caring for her. She cognitively produced a thought that supported her inner truth: "I don't deserve for people to love me and be warm to me."

Through this program she became aware of some startling realities. She thought about many of the wonderful people who wanted to become part of her life but whom she had rejected. She had found reasons to see those people as too needy and wanting too much of her time. They were giving and sweet, and as soon as they started to show these fine traits, Stacy's mental map took over.

She remembered one incident that was undeniably her way of throwing off any sense of warmth. Stacy shared that as a child, she hated her birthday because it always produced friction and fighting between her divorced parents. She was never given a party and would end up with a last-minute birthday cake with no friends to share it.

Shortly after graduating from college, Stacy's boyfriend threw a surprise birthday party for her and went to extremes to invite lots of people and have a fun evening. The whole event made Stacy furious. She was angry because he had invited some people who were not close friends. "How could he not know who my best friends were?" she wondered. She created a circumstance in which to be upset with him, instead of being thrilled by his thoughtfulness, because it was the way she had been programmed to feel about her birthday. Stacy's autopilot dictated that kindness made her uncomfortable and kept her involved with people who were quite the opposite.

Manage the Damage: Control

We all crave control; it's a natural instinct. When you are placed in an emotionally or physically dangerous position as a child, you are completely out of control. The mind can't manage it. It's a feeling that isn't easy to shake. As an adult, you still feel the need to deal with this past pain, and you do so by finding situations that remind you of the same feelings you had when you were young—except now you're dead set on getting control. You have the drive to conquer what you were unable to control as a child.

In many ways, this means you are flirting with danger. It can be a roller-coaster ride from which you might never get off.

TED'S STORY
Disaster Waiting to Happen

When Ted was a child, his family was destitute, not because his father didn't make a good living but because his father was a gambler. His mother screamed at his father daily about their living conditions, but it did nothing to change the family's circumstances. Finally at the end of her rope, Ted's mother ran off with another man and left Ted to be taken care of by his father. The betrayal caused Ted's father to add drinking to his vices.

Although Ted had no control over the financial crisis of his childhood, he did the best he could and took his first job at age fourteen. He endured until he was seventeen, then he left home and never looked back. Through an unusual series of circumstances, Ted started his own business, married, and started a family, and by his late twenties he was a millionaire. He was on easy street at last. That was until he leveraged everything, even his family's home, to move his business to the "next level." The recession hit, and his business venture failed miserably. He had to sell his house, move his family to a small apartment, and start his way back up the financial ladder.

Through this program, Ted discovered that he had brought disaster upon himself more than he had ever realized. He wasn't the first person to lose his shirt because of the recession, and he had plenty of reasons to believe that his financial downturn was out of his hands. However, going through the program made him realize that leveraging his house and everything else for a risky business venture was a seminal moment for him. He didn't have to do that. He now wonders what the "next level" even meant. After all, he already had plenty of money. Did he really need more? What was he trying to prove? If he had made it to the "next level," then what? He now believes he would have risked it all again.

In reality, Ted was acting like a small child out of control. When he made it financially, his mind needed him to flirt with being out of control all over again so that he could dig his way out and feel more in control, sending a message to the pained child that he was finally in control. Unfortunately, getting to the next level, whatever that may be, can never fill the void of a child who is desperately losing control. Even if Ted's effort had been successful, he would undoubtedly have continued to repeat the pattern to prove that he was mastering the feeling of being in control.

Take Back Your Life

Understanding what keeps you stuck in your childhood emotions is the key to figuring out how to walk away from them. That process starts now. This is what this step is all about. It begins with an awareness of the mindset of your childhood and the effect it has had on your life up until now. It's time to see yourself with a deeper understanding than you've ever had before. As you go through the journal exercises in this chapter, you will begin to see a pattern of life repeating itself—the effect of your parents' divorce on your life.

Imaging studies have demonstrated that the emotional center of the brain shows increased activity just before the cognitive center forms your actions and decisions. This suggests that everything we do is emotionally based. The cognitive brain develops logic to support the emotion driven by your mental map.

Stepping out of your past means changing the direction of your mental map and getting out of autopilot. It starts with seeing how you've unknowingly been duped into behaving a certain way. As this week unfolds, you will see how certain events have occurred and why you did certain things in order to reproduce unresolved childhood feelings. Your adult life is linked to your unhappy childhood, but it is revocable. Let's begin to break that bond.

You will reflect on the effect of your parents' divorce in two stages: In part 1 you will reflect on events of your life that have not gone well. For instance, maybe you did badly in college and, as a result, have never been able to get the type of meaningful work you've always desired. Maybe you screwed up one love relationship after another. Or maybe you're so introverted that you spend too much time alone and feel lonesome.

In part 2 you will recall actions and inactions that you regret and have always wished you could take back. For instance, perhaps you didn't communicate well with a past lover who left you, or maybe you've had difficulty being close to your children in the way you want. Maybe you have cheated on a spouse or have allowed someone to continue to hurt you.

Remember that the mind can be tricky; what's most meaningful and potentially the most helpful may be hiding in the recesses of your mind. So be patient. Advance through this step slowly, working on different events each day. If you find yourself having any anxiety, turn your journal to a fresh page and record how you are feeling. Take it one day and one event at a time. By the end of the week you will have linked your past to your present life with a new understanding that will take you to the next level of change.

If you have trouble getting started or getting through part 1, the real-life examples that follow part 2 can serve as a model and give you a clearer idea of how to proceed.

Journal Exercise: My Life, Part 1

Through the eyes of a child, adults are a powerful entity. Parents are (or at least are supposed to be) role models. Teachers are authority figures. Every action, word, emotion, and expression conveyed from a grown-up to a child is absorbed and interpreted. All of these adults have a powerful effect on the events of life as you grow up.

Your main task this week is to draw on these events and interpret them. This is a means to understand how the messages of your childhood have led you to unwittingly behave in certain ways in certain situations and have gotten you involved in events or with people that, in hindsight, you know you should have avoided.

In this part, write down five of the most obvious and meaningful examples from your life in each of the following four categories. Whatever you feel, it is important to get it all in writing. Leave some empty space, at least ten lines, after each of the twenty events that you will recollect, because you will be coming back to them. Here are the four categories:

1. *Unhappy childhood or adolescent events.* These should be events in which one or both of your parents did something that directly affected you in a negative way. You may include unhappy experiences that occurred in school, camp, or elsewhere, if you can connect them to your parents' divorce. Try to avoid repeating the memories you recorded in chapter 4, if possible.

2. *Unhappy adult events.* Do not think of these in terms of your parents. Just recall the unhappiest times of your life after you left home.

3. *Things or feelings I wish I hadn't done or felt in childhood or adolescence.* The intention here is to bring up any and all events for which you'd like to take back an action or a feeling.

4. *Things or feelings I wish I hadn't done or felt in adulthood.* Again, bring up the unfortunate mistakes you have made or felt throughout adulthood.

After recording five experiences in each category, write down and answer, after each one, "How I felt during and after this event."

Journal Exercise: My Life, Part 2

This part is the link that will help you understand that the childhood feelings you experienced pushed you to experience the same feelings during events that occurred in your adult life. By matching the two sets of feelings and experiences, you will begin to see how familiar you are with these feelings and will understand that it is not a coincidence that you have continued to experience them throughout life.

Now we are going to return to the journal list you began in part 1 and fill in the rest of the blank lines under each item. Now that you understand how your mind can work against you, you are going to start the task of making it work for you. Write down and complete these two statements:

1. *This reminds me of the following childhood feelings, experiences, and messages sent to me about myself:* How were you made to *feel* as a child, and how does it relate to each of the events you wrote about? Fill in the blank lines by writing about that childhood time and the feelings that remind you of the experience you listed.

2. *My new insight about this link:* Don't worry about getting it exactly right. Just allow yourself to think aloud and consider various possibilities. Remember that you may have one childhood feeling and experience that you link to more than one adult feeling and experience. It's okay to use that childhood feeling or experience multiple times to explain why certain things happened or you did certain things throughout your life.

Your journal in step 3 should look like this example for each of the five events in the four categories:

Unhappy adult event #1

_____

_____

_____

_____

_____

_____

How I felt during and after this event

_____

_____

_____

_____

_____

This reminds me of the following childhood feelings, experiences, or messages sent to me about myself:

_____

_____

_____

_____

_____

My new insight about this link:

_____

_____

_____

_____

_____

To show you how this works in real life, I'd like to introduce you to Tim.

How Divorce Affected Tim

Tim is a self-proclaimed "middle-aged worrywart." He has two teenage children and a loving and devoted wife. He's been selling commercial real estate for twenty years and has been quite successful. Even though he loves his job and would never want to change professions, he has way too much pent-up tension from wondering when he'll sign up a new listing and make his next sale. This tension has even landed him in the emergency room.

"My constant worry is overwhelming me," he wrote, "and it came to a head when I went to the emergency room recently, thinking I was having a heart attack. I was sure of it, and my wife and kids were terrified. I felt like a complete fool when the doctor told me I needed antianxiety medication and the name of a good psychiatrist. He warned me that I already had high blood pressure and was going to give myself an ulcer if I didn't get help."

Tension had become a way of life for Tim, but he didn't realize just how much his feelings of insecurity that started with his parents' divorce were affecting virtually every aspect of his life.

The next section consists of verbatim excerpts from Tim's journal.

Tim's Journal

Tim's Unhappy Childhood or Adolescent Event #1: I Hated Having to Go to Camp

Going to summer camp when I was eight. I was too afraid to talk to anyone and too shy to participate in the activities. Of course, I wouldn't dare approach a girl that I might've liked. I would see other boys congregating and would just sit there, pretending to be reading while I was imagining what it might be like to be included as part of the group. They even referred to me as the "worm" because I was a bookworm. Little did they know that I barely read. I stared into the pages and turned them every few minutes to make it look like I was reading, thinking I wanted to be anywhere but where I was.

How I felt during and after this event: Nervous, insecure. It was like life was happening around me, and I wasn't part of it. Now I can see how my childhood made me feel so out of control that I lived all of my life feeling like I was staring at it from the outside looking in.

This reminds me of the following childhood feelings, experiences, or messages sent to me about myself: I often didn't feel secure at home because all the fighting and uncertainty at home made me nervous and insecure. You just freeze up as a kid. You know this is horrible. You can't stand it and you want to stop it but you can't. So you cry, then you hide and you feel like a dope because you're so weak. If I let myself just go there even now, I get knots in my stomach. I can literally feel the anxiety in me as I write this, as if I might start shaking.

My new insight about this link: So going away from home to an unknown environment was even worse. Instead of being on vacation from my crappy home and feeling free, I took all of the anxiety and hopelessness with me. I was the same kid at camp: scared and nervous. I should've been able to say to myself that I was a pretty neat kid. I had interesting thoughts, liked sports, and knew a lot about my hometown teams. I'd hear kids discussing sports in groups and think to myself all of the opinions and facts I could express, but I was still that little kid at home standing frozen, hearing fighting and feeling like I had no power. I had no power; that's the insight I'm coming to realize about myself.

Tim's Unhappy Childhood or Adolescent Event #2: I Was Shunned as a Child

In seventh grade a group of my friends stopped talking to me. For no reason. They just stopped. I was miserable and sick about it, but I never asked why or confronted them. When they started speaking to me the following year, I was too afraid to ask them why they had stopped talking to me.

How I felt during and after this event: I was afraid to bring up anything that might upset my "friends" and might make them stop talking to me again. So when I did get my friends back, I was too worried and uncomfortable to ask them what went wrong.

This reminds me of the following childhood feelings, experiences, or messages sent to me about myself: My parents constantly fought, and I often felt nervous to bring up any conflict. Plus, I saw how they handled conflict between themselves.

My new insight about this link: At home, confrontation often ended with people being angry and my mom storming out and leaving us. So I guess that's why I was afraid to confront my friends. Maybe I thought they would act like my mom and possibly leave.

Tim's Unhappy Adult Event #1: Not Being Able to Commit to Marriage Sooner

I dated my wife on and off for eight years. I couldn't commit, and I wouldn't even tell her I loved her, though I did. We would break up frequently and I'd keep asking her to take me back. For some reason, she did. Every time. However, I was always too afraid to ask her where we stood or if we had a future. I just couldn't be straightforward about my feelings. I loved her, but I was unable to take control of my life and this relationship. I preferred to let the relationship end rather than have an honest conversation about how I felt about her and make myself vulnerable. Ultimately, I finally walked away from the relationship, and then down the line we ended up happily married.

How I felt during and after this event: I couldn't ask what was going on with her feelings, either. I was so afraid of rejection, I couldn't bear to hear her say anything other than she wanted me. So instead, I avoided the simple conversation that any other man would have with the love of his life. I could've lost her forever, because I couldn't muster up the courage to have a clear conversation about our relationship. I couldn't handle hearing her say she really didn't love me, so I never asked. I let the status quo go on way too long because of my fears.

This reminds me of the following childhood feelings, experiences, or messages sent to me about myself: I remember when I kind of felt the same "in limbo" feeling when my parents told us they were getting a divorce, but then it was almost a year before they actually decided to do it. During that whole time my sister and I had no idea where it stood, and every day I felt almost panicked. Would my mom leave? Would my parents divorce? What would happen?

My new insight about this link: Maybe I didn't ask my wife how she felt about me or if she loved me because I was afraid of the answer. When I was a child and my mom left for a few months before the divorce, I felt rejected by her. Maybe I feared my wife would reject me the same way she did.

Tim's Unhappy Adult Event #2: Blowing an Incident out of Proportion

Early in my marriage, I had a legal issue with a traffic violation—very high speeding mixed with letting my insurance lapse. It worried me for nine months. I feared I would lose my job and our finances, and I actually totally fell apart until the issue was resolved. I simply couldn't cope—I couldn't eat or sleep or think of anything else. It was totally unreasonable. But I could've gotten a lot of points on my license, and in my mind, if that happened, I was one speeding ticket away from losing my license. I was so frustrated and angry with myself for getting this ticket that I let it drive me crazy. How stupid could I be? I'd imagine my boss finding out and firing me for being irresponsible and not an upright citizen. As I write it, I can see how crazy it seems and that it wasn't logical. Now I can see it was just my regular anxiety and need to be afraid of something, and this served that purpose well.

How I felt during and after this event: I was consumed with worry and feeling out of control. The whole thing became much bigger in my head than it actually was.

This reminds me of the following childhood feelings, experiences, or messages sent to me about myself: As a child I felt so out of control with the divorce. Specifically, not knowing for a year if my parents would divorce at all. It was the worst feeling. Somehow the not knowing made everything feel like it was spinning out of control. I was tied up in knots for the entire year, overcome with worry over what would happen to my family and if it would break apart.

My new insight about this link: Maybe the fear of the unknown for so long regarding my parents' divorce (and whether we'd be a family or not) pushed its way into my adult life. (This traffic violation became a replay of that year as a kid when I was constantly worrying. I took that traffic violation and made a mountain out of a molehill. All of a sudden, I was worried, unjustly, that it would cause my whole world to change. Perhaps my wife and work would be devastated. Now I'm realizing that it was a ridiculous fear, but it was the same fear of losing everything I had as a child for that whole year. I took the same fears and placed them on top of this new adult situation and felt the same threat: the idea that this traffic violation could define my life (like the divorce) and I just had to wait and wait (like my parents' decision about the divorce). Maybe the reason I couldn't cope was that it reminded me of the feelings I had when I was a kid.

Tim's Unhappy Adult Event #3: Going to Law School Was a Mistake

After college, I wasn't sure what I wanted to do, so I attended law school only because I got good LSAT scores and my father encouraged me to go. I had no feelings inside about what I wanted to do. I was lost—smart but lost. I didn't have the value and power inside to know what I wanted to do. In order to make my father happy, I went to law school. After about three weeks, I realized this was not for me and I left school, totally against my father's wishes, and I was so ashamed.

How I felt during and after this event: Ashamed that I had let my father down. (Once again, I was a failure.)

This reminds me of the following childhood feelings, experiences, or messages sent to me about myself: Afraid of disappointing my parents, not being good enough.

My new insight about this link: I was afraid of making any mistakes, so I just did what my parents thought I should do, even if it wasn't for me.

Tim's Things or Feelings He Wishes He Hadn't Done or Felt in Childhood or Adolescence #1: Saying Hurtful Words

I remember when I was about nine years old I got so enraged with a friend—frankly, I don't even remember why—that I said an awful thing to him. His father had passed away and I told him, "At least I have a father; yours is dead."

How I felt during and after this event: I was so angry inside from what was going on in my home, and I just wanted to hurt someone. I didn't dare speak up at home about my real hurt or anger, so I had to find someone else to push these feelings onto. And I went for the jugular.

This reminds me of the following childhood feelings, experiences, or messages sent to me about myself: I was insecure and unhappy because my parents were fighting all of the time.

My new insight about this link: I was filled with so much rage at my parents that I just had to pin it on someone.

Tim's Things or Feelings He Wishes He Hadn't Done or Felt in Childhood or Adolescence #2: I Was Too Shy in High School

I wish I could have approached others in high school. I spent all of high school skipping lunch and sitting near the football field because I was so uncomfortable in the cafeteria with all the groups of kids. I couldn't have any real conversation with anyone and was especially nervous if there was a group.

How I felt during and after this event: Uncomfortable. I knew the other kids would reject me. Now I realize that it made no sense. I wasn't different from them, and I had just as interesting things to say, but it didn't matter. In my mind they'd find some reason to not like me. Being from a divorced home made me feel like a freak. So why bother?

This reminds me of the following childhood feelings, experiences, or messages sent to me about myself: I was so insecure with myself, it wasn't worth the risk of rejection. I would rather sit by myself and stare out into space rather than engage in a conversation and try to fit in.

My new insight about this link: I was constantly afraid of my parents' rejection, and I think that carried over to the same fear with my peers.

Tim's Things or Feelings He Wishes He Hadn't Done or Felt in Childhood or Adolescence #3: Fighting with My Sister

I regret the horrible physical fights I had with my sister. I would rage so much that she was actually afraid of me.

How I felt during and after this event: Terribly angry and out of control.

This reminds me of the following childhood feelings, experiences, or messages sent to me about myself: Everything in our home was out of control. I was at least going to control things with her. If she made me mad, I was determined not to let her get away with it.

My new insight about this link: I feel bad that my sister and I fought, even though it only occurred for a short time. I guess I did it because I wanted to feel empowered and not like I was just some little kid who had no control.

Tim's Things or Feelings He Wishes He Hadn't Done or Felt in Adulthood #1: Yelling at My Baby Daughter

When my son was just born and my daughter was about fifteen months old, she woke up crying and woke him up. My wife was out of town at a conference, and I got so upset that my daughter woke up the baby that I yelled at her to shut up. She was just a baby herself, yet I got so angry at her and really lost control. I still feel very guilty about that.

How I felt during and after this event: I felt totally out of control. I couldn't handle one baby waking up the other. At the time, both of them crying in the middle of the night while I was alone with them seemed like an impossible situation.

This reminds me of the following childhood feelings, experiences, or messages sent to me about myself: Sometimes my parents would fight so loud in the middle of the night that I'd actually think the screaming was loud enough to make the roof cave in.

My new insight about this link: Maybe being alone in the house with a screaming child reminded me of myself as a little boy under the covers wishing my parents would just stop yelling.

Tim's Things or Feelings He Wishes He Hadn't Done or Felt in Adulthood #2: Acting Intolerant during a Family Crisis

My nephew was fifteen, and he had to stay with us because his mother (my sister) was suffering from depression and had been hospitalized for a mental illness. I was never patient enough or tolerant of my nephew during the nine months he was staying with me while my sister was in treatment.

How I felt during and after this event: Having this crisis of mental illness with my sister made me so uncomfortable. I chose to become irritable and overwhelmed instead of being more adult about it.

This reminds me of the following childhood feelings, experiences, or messages sent to me about myself: It reminded me of the times in our childhood when she would become manic, then depressed, and I hated everything about that time.

My new insight about this link: Maybe having my nephew in my house reminded me too much of my childhood turmoil with the divorce. He was also a constant reminder that I had a sister with a mental illness, which was putting a stress on all of us. I was angry about it.

Tim's Things or Feelings He Wishes He Hadn't Done or Felt in Adulthood #3: Fear of Failing

I waste a lot of my time worrying about things—especially things like money. What if something happens and we have nothing? It terrifies me. My fears are not normal. My financial issues are nothing unusual. Anybody could lose everything at any moment. But for me, instead of being able to focus on how much money I have and the stable job I have, I typically focus on what could go wrong and why I should never get financially comfortable.

How I felt during and after this event: I'm always worried that "the other shoe is going to drop." Financial worries never even came about until I had kids. Now I worry about money a lot. I'm afraid that something could happen and I would be unable to care for them and give them the normal childhood that I missed having.

This reminds me of the following childhood feelings, experiences, or messages sent to me about myself: I was always worrying as a kid: Will mom come back, is dad still depressed, will my sister go into a rage? I felt like everything was my responsibility.

My new insight about this link: Now that I'm an adult, I still worry. I'm afraid of things spinning out of control and that I'll be left with that same empty feeling. I'm terrified I will not be able to control my children's world, in the same way that my childhood was out of control. Now I finally can understand that I'm just applying my childhood fears into my daily adult world and I don't have to do that.

Understanding Equals Control

As you can see, Tim was working hard to try to have a much deeper understanding of why his life turned out the way it did. As he personally confronted his issues and actions, he could see how his past had dictated how his life unfolded. This understanding gave him a renewed control over his life because he could finally see that he, and not the messages from his past, was in control. Your understanding will do the same for you.

The Parent Letter

The parent letter is one of the most important exercises of the program. Its effect can be enormous. In addition to the other journal exercises you are doing in this chapter, I would like you to write a letter to each of your parents independently, speaking your truth and letting each parent know how his or her behavior has made you feel.

This letter is *not* meant to be sent, given, or read to your parents—ever. It should not be written or edited with the intention of it being seen by anyone. As you write, don't be concerned about your sentences being grammatically correct or whether you're meandering. I want you to write in your stream of consciousness. Just let it out and say all at once what you now know about how their divorce has affected your life.

Even if you have done this or something similar before, do it again, because this time you've allowed yourself to really dig deep and find new, insightful ways of understanding your life. Tell each parent how his or her behavior has affected your life as a child and as an adult. Let both of them know how you feel as you're writing it.

For once, be completely open and honest with your parents and yourself. Tell them how you're going to change, take back your life, and take control.

If you feel a need to say something nice, go right ahead. Many people feel a need to start off with something like "I know you love me and tried your best, but I've recently discovered . . ." You can include all the good times you had as well.

Remember, you are doing this just for you. You need to have a moment in time when you can release your feelings and be heard by the person who is most important to you right now: *you*. As you'll find out in the next step, you are going to need to understand and care for yourself from this point onward. For now, however, it is important to write these letters with no barriers to what goes in them.

Writing these letters does not have to be done in any particular order in this chapter. It's just important that you write them this week, before you proceed to the next step. Also, put at least a day between the first and second letter. Too much emotion is being spent to write these letters back-to-back.

When you're ready to write, find a quiet time and space. Many people find that a good time is later in the evening when the rest of the house has quieted down. This allows you to open up and let loose with your internal dialogue.

I found these two sets of letters from people in my research group particularly moving. The writers were happy to share them in the hope that they will inspire you to get your own personal thoughts on paper.

Dear Mom,

As I go deeper with my healing, I am learning ways that I am scarred. I know you did the best that you could, and I truly understand that now. I know the ways in which you were scarred as a child and know that you didn't know any better. You didn't know how to truly show me love, acceptance, and confidence, because you lacked those things yourself.

However, as a result of not receiving these things from you, I suffer from feelings of occasional depression, low self-worth, poor self-image, and failed relationships. It is very difficult for me to trust people and also for me to determine who is worthy of my trust. Often, I have chosen to trust people who were unworthy and have allowed myself to be in relationships that have caused me great harm. But I do not believe the damage is irreparable. That's why I am trying so hard to be a better person—for me first and then for my children. Your grandchildren.

I now know that I have always been looking for a mother figure. As a child, it seems as though I understood this more clearly. I looked to people like Ms. Jamison [a teacher] to tell me I was loved, lovely, and worthy of good things. This was not her responsibility, and I was harmed as a result. I looked to men to tell me good things about myself. I thought that I had to repay them for their "kindness" with my time and my body. It was and is a vicious cycle, one in which a part of me and my self-worth erodes further with each and every encounter.

I forgive you for these areas in which you failed me as a parent. I forgive myself for abusing my body and letting others do the same. I forgive myself for allowing others to have the most sacred parts of me—my body, my mind, my time and energy—when they were undeserving of it. I forgive myself for not being mindful with the way I spent money. I forgive myself for taking friendships and real love for granted when offered. I forgive myself for not seeing people as they are when they present themselves to me. Actions say a lot about a person's character. My character has not always presented itself in the best way. It has taken a long time to develop, and I know I have made great strides toward becoming a healthy person who truly loves herself, loves God, and is able to love others in return.

I cannot say that I truly love myself yet. I do feel I am on the right path toward doing so. I cannot say that I truly love anyone other than my children. In time, I pray that I will be able to have love for myself and others—including you. It is a necessity, but I will only take it if it is a healthy love.

I forgive you. I know this is a work in progress, but I am excited about my progress thus far.

Love,

Linda

Dear Dad,

I wish you could look at yourself and not blame me for not wanting to be part of your life when I was a child. I had to protect myself from the hurt. You say you fought to have me full-time and that this action should have proved your love for me. But I knew your reasons for wanting full custody, and it was not from the viewpoint of a loving parent. You were selfish and only wanted to punish my mom. You then chose to make a new family and try to get me to fit into it instead of honoring your firstborn.

You fought over paying minimal child support yet made three more babies. I hate money battles to this day because I witnessed the evils of money. You are cheap and held money over my head. When I no longer needed your money, I was free. I was free of the conditional love. I was the kid without the father from ages twenty to thirty because you chose to honor your new family's needs before mine. Yet you act like the victim! You act like the sad wounded one and put all the blame on what you call "forces." Those forces were you, your wife, and my mom. You were the adult and I was the child. You were the one who made the choices of how you would act during and after the divorce. I had no say in anything and yet you blame me, the child. How?

I don't want to hear the stories from the past anymore about how my mom did this or how you tried to do this or that. You change your reality and fail to understand what mine is and was. Our realities are so different that we will never understand each other's truths, but we could start fresh. We could make a new relationship built on trust and honesty. In order to do that, you need to hear me and acknowledge who is the child and who is the adult.

Your daughter,

Linda

Mom,

Your rigidness and inability to open up and share things with us made my childhood very difficult. I do know that you did your best and that you love us very much. However, all of your fighting with Dad when I was younger was terrifying, unsettling, and horrible. I do not think you should have exposed us to that. I never felt secure. I never felt peace.

Our house was not a comfortable place to be from the time I was about eight years old. My memories consist of a lot of fighting.

When you decided to get a divorce and then tell us about it, you never actually went ahead and got the divorce—but you neglected to tell us what the hell was going on. I lived in limbo for a year—too afraid to ask what was going on and making up my own worst truth. I was frequently unhappy and anxious, and I really didn't have the ability to have the kind of fun kids should.

I think you were way too interested in getting your master's [degree] and working on your PhD than having us around. When you and Dad got divorced and you let him move back in the house (you moved to a dorm), it felt like you left to get away from us so you could study. Then when you and Dad were back together, when I was in high school, you moved to a different state to finish your PhD courses. That felt like you abandoned me. We had just moved to a new state and started at a new school, and you took off. Even though I was angry and didn't like authority, you should have been there.

I wish things with you didn't have to be all or nothing. You got remarried to Dad within three years; why didn't you just get separated and not put us through all that? You should have known how all of your crap was affecting Samantha and me. I think you were very selfish. At the very least, you should have been open about every step and told us what was going on. The stuff I created in my head was so much worse. I think you have come a long way and are a much better communicator than you used to be, only I wish you had been that way when I was a kid.

The good news is, I intend to keep the lines of communication open with my own kids so they don't ever have to have sad, secret thoughts and worries like I did. I know that you probably didn't know better—or you would have done better.

I deal with a lot of worries as an adult, but I will work on understanding why I feel this way, and I will learn how to cope with it in an effective way.

I hope you know how much I love you.

Tony

Dad,

I think you were a total and complete rage-aholic when I was a kid. If you didn't lose your temper so much, Mom would not have wanted a divorce. You would get mad at her and Samantha and you would lose control. Although you got angry with me a lot less than you did them, I was still terrified of you losing your temper. I felt like I needed to keep you happy so you wouldn't get angry with anyone.

When you and Mom decided to get a divorce, you never talked to us about it at all. You got sad and depressed but really didn't let us know what was going on. I think that was very unfair to Sam and me. Why wouldn't you or Mom let us know what was going on? This affected our lives. We knew there were problems and were not free to discuss any of it. It was a horrible and unsettling feeling.

I think the two of you had an obligation to get along and work things out. You had absolutely no right to scream and fight in front of us. It was like living in a war zone. We were children; you should have had more self-control. Both of you should have.

I never knew if you were in a good mood or a bad mood, and what mood you were in dictated how the day was at our house.

Then you got divorced, and I know how depressed you were. I felt so sorry for you, and there was nothing I could do to make you happy. I think that as a parent you should have been stronger for me and communicated with me. When a kid doesn't know what's going on in the family, it is frightening. I never knew what to expect next—even when you decided to remarry each other, you told us just matter-of-fact. Don't you know the shit I went through with you two fighting and separating and divorcing? It was a terrible thing that happened to me—I felt extremely unsafe and insecure. Then you are just up and remarrying each other?

Now today I am so happy our family is complete—but then, I wish you had had more insight about how you two were affecting us. You cannot have the same anniversary date and pretend that the divorce never happened. You cannot deny it—it was a monumental thing for me, and I will never forget the pain I felt.

Your son,

Tony

A Conversation with Your Child Within

Imagine what would have happened if someone came to you as a child and explained everything that you are now coming to understand about your childhood and its effect on you. Life could have been so much different. If only an adult had sat you down and told you that it didn't have to be this way, that you didn't have to take in all of this hurt and allow it to become part of your internal self. If someone had explained to you the truth—that what was going on around you wasn't about you, and it wasn't for you to personalize every ounce of it and create an identity through it—you'd be a different person today.

But that didn't happen. That person didn't exist—until now. *You* are that adult who can reach back and give the child still within permission to live life over in a new way that includes a truer identity.

Before you can begin to change—before you move on to the final step—you need to have that conversation with yourself and free the child within from the limitations of certain negative childhood messages.

Again, to make this useful, there is a best way to go about it: On a sunny afternoon, grab your journal, go outside to a place where you are in nature (a field, a lake, among trees) and can be alone. Imagine that you happen upon yourself as a child sitting comfortably on a bench. Imagine going over to that child, putting your arm around him or her, and telling what you now know. Tell this child everything you need for him or her to know. Lovingly explain that it's not his or her fault, that the child doesn't deserve what's happening or is about to happen, and that he or she is worthy. Sincerely connect with your life as a kid. Give the child within permission to see the world differently than he or she has been made to believe. Then take your journal and write down the dialogue that you imagine would take place.

Consider what the child might say and how he or she might respond to you. The child might not believe you, and you will have to be convincing. How would you do that? What will you say when he or she doesn't believe you? Write it down, either as you're having the dialogue, or right after you have imagined it. Finally, when you are finished, write down how it felt to truly connect with that little person.

Here's an example of what the conversation might be like. It comes from a woman in my research group named Kate:

> First I would hug that little girl; a real, real hug that says how much she is loved. Then I'd say, "You are sweet, beautiful, and smart. I know you don't believe what you are being told. When your daddy yells and scares you, it really isn't because you're bad at all. That time he shoved you against the wall—it wasn't you! You could never do anything to deserve that! Don't you see how he is angry all the time with everyone? Look at how he treats your brother, who you know is not bad, either.
>
> Your mom and dad fight because they have problems. They can't get along. They were probably fighting before you were born, because it has *nothing to do with you!!* You look in the mirror and feel ugly and unable to talk, but you are pretty and your words are beautiful. You will know this years from now, but for now just believe that you are worth being loved. Tell yourself you will grow up and find love and find happiness. Tell yourself you are beautiful inside and out.
>
> How it makes me feel to connect with my child self: This makes me and little me feel good. If only someone would have given me the opportunity to share my fears as a kid. That would have been such a relief.

Get Ready for Change

You now have a true understanding of who you are not and who you can become. You are now ready to change. You have opened your heart to the possibilities of being whoever you wish to be. Now you are in control. You are set to begin the journey of discovering who you really want to be now that you have freed yourself from the past and are limitless.

6

Create Change
in Your Life

Step 4, Weeks 4 and 5

Change—ask any adults what they think of it, and most will say they hate it. Making and accepting change is a very hard thing to do. Instinctively, virtually everybody resists it. I hear people say all the time, "I can't change who I am."

The reason is that it forces them to get out of autopilot. The mental map that sets a person's course in life is so powerful that it seems too overwhelming to change it. In fact, the closest most people come to change is when an outside influence—be it a traffic citation, a warning from the doctor, or a poor performance review—forces them to behave in a different way. It's a valiant effort and surely works, but only to a limited degree. The persistent struggle to change eventually catches up with them, and in a moment of weakness the old behavior returns. They start driving too fast again. They go back to eating the wrong things. Or they start up the old habit of turning their work in late.

I had a friend who was overweight and out of shape and began jogging to better manage his health. Every day he went through his routine, and every day it was an incredible struggle for him. Nothing unusual there—he just had to keep pushing. And push he did. For three months, five days a week, he kept at it. He was losing weight, but he was not happy. He finally shared his frustration with me. The exercise never got any easier, he lamented. He complained that he was always out of breath after the first five minutes, and the rest of the workout was grueling.

It didn't make sense. The whole idea of jogging is to build up your endurance so you can go farther and faster. Eventually he just ran out of energy and stopped working out, so I suggested he see a doctor. Sure enough, he had a congenital heart problem that was causing the exhaustion. His doctor prescribed medication to control the condition and had him follow an exercise regimen that fit his disorder. Soon he was feeling good, losing weight, and building endurance.

Facing change is similar to what my friend went through. Making the change you want in life requires extreme mental energy every day, and there will be times when you're going to feel that fitting into your new behavior never gets any easier. The forces that fight you siphon off your energy, making you feel like you've run out of gas. It's the reason so many people think they can't really change who they are. They make some effort that never seems to get easier. They run out of energy, cave in, and revert to their old ways. They rationalize that going against the grain just doesn't make sense. Their belief that they can't change is supported by the fact that their efforts don't seem to get any easier. There's always an internal force pulling them back like a magnet.

Becoming Change

In order for change to take root, it has to become part of you. It can't be just an act you're trying to portray. Change is *you*. It means changing every fiber of your being. Every time you do something different, you will be redrawing your mental map, little by little. It will take time and effort. But sure enough, you'll gradually find that it becomes easier to behave differently in whatever way you desire. The struggle will diminish because your effort will no longer be going against the grain. Like the beltway that avoids big-city traffic jams, your mental map will be redirected to bypass the pain of the past. The changed you will become the new Main Street of your mental map.

No longer will you be on autopilot feeling bound and chained to your issues; rather, you will feel freed from it all and open to new ideas and ways to live your life. It will *become* your life, the one you own and want.

This doesn't mean that you won't struggle. But your struggle will be with clarity and the knowledge of a plan for the person you want to become. It will be directed at developing a new you, someone devoid of the issues that have always hampered you from creating the life you want.

People who say, "I am who I am" do not understand the process of change. It doesn't work like magic or hypnosis. You won't be changing anything about yourself that you like. You will concentrate on what you don't like: your negative mindset and attitude of doom that prevents you from achieving what you want in life.

Because you now wisely understand the connection between your past and your present, every moment of change will include a deeper understanding of yourself. You will finally get to know yourself and be able to decide what you want your own truth to be. You might have to search a bit to discover it, but you *will* find it, and it will become part of you.

Parent Yourself

One part of getting over your childhood involves the concept of parenting yourself. You can't go backward and reinvent the past. You can't change your parents and the environment in which you were raised. You can't rewrite history. Yet you need to feed yourself the messages of worthiness that you deserved to receive as a child. You will do this by learning how to parent yourself.

As a loving parent, you'd be downright hostile if someone suggested your child was worthless. Now you will be the loving parent of yourself. When you feel your autopilot pounding negative messages into your head, you will stand up as your own protective parent and tell yourself what you think of that disgusting thought. Just because you didn't have a parent to protect you as a child doesn't mean you can't have one now. Be your own parent and protect and direct yourself with the messages you deserve to hear. Parenting yourself will lead you to a natural feeling of love and kindness toward yourself.

Adopt an Attitude of Awareness

When you surmount a series of challenges, you attain permanent change. The biggest challenge you must surmount is your autopilot. Being on autopilot means you're not consciously thinking about your behavior and responses to everyday life, so you must adopt a mindset of awareness. This means you must be cognizant of how you are feeling and behaving at all times. You have to be alert for the tendency to start drifting back into autopilot.

Think of it as a relaxation tape that suggests you focus on your breathing. You can't change your breathing, slow it down, or take deeper breaths until you become consciously aware of your breathing in the first place. How often do you pay attention to your breathing? Almost never. It's automatic, and you can't change its pattern unless you start to take moments in your day to purposely focus on it. To realize change, you have to do the same with your emotions.

The challenge will always be to prevent your mental map from taking you to those familiar places in childhood and from convincing you that this is where you belong. Don't just accept your feelings in any given situation; rather, challenge your mental map. Courageously test yourself to see if you have to feel or act the way your mind is telling you to feel or act in certain situations. Consider why you would feel or act that way and immediately compare it to what you've learned about your truth.

Can you link your behavior to your upbringing and see how you might feel a certain way as a result of your parents' divorce and/or related issues? Trust me, if it's a feeling you've evaluated as doing you no good, it's related somehow to your childhood. Investigate and identify it. Once you've found it, you have to recognize that even though you'd like to give in to the impulse of your autopilot, you're going to force the change with your new-found deep knowledge.

This gives you the control to create the life you want. Control comes from a deeper knowledge of self that gives you the power to act and feel as you desire instead of being tied to a set of rules and regulations made by others. With this control, you are able to create a new reality that comes from within you and that you can evaluate without the complications of painful or conflicted feelings from your past.

The Change Process

1. Focus on daily emotions and behavior—control.
2. Would you like to feel differently?
3. How is it linked to childhood truth?

4. Allow (push) yourself to feel or act differently—create.
5. Say your new truth aloud.

Select What You Want to Change

Children of divorce are left with a lot of emotional fallout that follows them through life, like radiation from a nuclear meltdown. My research shows that everyone's story is different, but the effects are very similar. Below is a list of the most common emotional traits that befall a child of divorce.

Before you get started on this important step, take time to review this list. Use it to help you draw out your feelings about the unhappy circumstances in your life. As you review this list, consider which traits you most want to change and write them down in your journal. These are the emotions and circumstances of your life that you will be working on changing in this chapter. Feel free to add others that do not appear on this list. No list is too long.

These are the most common emotional traits in children of divorce:

Low self-confidence

Low self-worth

Guilt

Loneliness

Instability and a feeling of being lost

Money worries

Unfaithfulness in marriage

Inability to sustain a love relationship

Lack of trust in others and/or oneself

Persistent sadness, anxiety, or depression

Inability to communicate feelings

Avoidance of confrontation

Lack of emotion or a sense of feeling numb

Taking a sense of responsibility to extremes

Quickness to anger, prone to fighting

Self-doubt about one's own parenting skills

Write Your Daily Mission Statement

You're going to start the process of change by creating a mission statement about how you desire to see each day in your life unfold. How do you want to envision your day, and how do you fit into it? What do you want to feel emotionally? What must you do to accomplish your daily mission?

Many people keep a mission statement in their minds. It's often something simple like "Today I want to be happy, in love." But then they do nothing to make it happen. They do not plan downtime to chat and laugh with their spouses, spend time doing something enjoyable with their children, or do anything that would bring happiness to themselves. Then when it doesn't happen, they're upset that their day didn't turn out the way they wanted it to be.

If you want to feel love today, what are you going to do to make that happen? Write it down. If your mission is to take care of and be kind to yourself today, how do you plan to do that, exactly? Write it down. When you see it in black and white, it's easier to fight your mental map.

Each day brings new trials and situations, and your mission statement will help you to anticipate and plan for them. If today you have to take your sick child to the doctor, work overtime, cook for a holiday dinner, or deal with your taxes, what will your mission statement be for that day? How will you approach the day to fit the new mental map that you have chosen?

You no longer want to be affected by your past truth. Starting your day with a mission statement will help you to avert this.

Do Emotional Checkups

Change involves constantly checking in with your emotions. At least twice a day you will need to make this process formal through journal writing. The primary checkup will always be at the end of the day. This is when you will review and consider many of your daily issues and feelings and write about them in your journal. In addition, take a measure of how your day is going at least one other time during the day and write about it. Noon or lunchtime is a good time, but do it whenever you can steal away for a few minutes and take time for yourself.

Preferably, you should check in with your emotions many times throughout the day, just to measure how your new mental map is taking hold. You don't want the old one sneaking up on you! The more frequently you check in, the easier it is to get off autopilot. If you start slipping, the emotional checkup is a reminder to adjust.

Don't make excuses that allow you to gloss over this step. Your emotional checkups are crucial because they are a way of telling your autopilot that you're not giving in. Simply ask yourself, "How am I feeling at the moment? Is this how I want to feel? Is my behavior what I truly want from myself?" Make note of your answers in your journal. Consider how the behavior relates to your past and what you've learned about it so that you can change the pattern of your day immediately. Take note of your feelings throughout the day so that you can think and write about them in more depth at the end of the day.

Writing everything down in the moment is important for staying honest with yourself. Otherwise, it'll be like waking up in the middle of the night from a dream so vivid that you tell yourself you're bound to remember it in the morning. But lo and behold, when you awake again in the morning, it's gone.

Patience and Diligence

Change calls for very deep mental and emotional work. You must be diligent about it or else your autopilot will try to sneak in and take over. If you do not work diligently, you won't change. Writing your feelings down will force you to remember exactly how you felt and what was going on around you at the time. You need to do this in order to seriously consider how your behavior is tapping into your mental map. Only then can you create change for tomorrow.

The Beginning of Change

Every day for the next two weeks, create a mission statement and write it down in your journal on a new page. Below each mission statement, do your emotional checkup by writing down and answering these questions:

- Did I need to feel or behave the way I did?
- Would I have wanted to feel or behave differently?
- How do I wish I would have felt or behaved differently?
- What feelings or issues from my past would have possibly motivated me to feel or behave the way I did?

Be creative. If you're not exactly sure how to answer these questions, then write down as many possibilities as come to mind. It may not be just one thing; many issues and feelings from your past may have conspired to give your autopilot the message that you "should" feel or behave a certain way. Use the time to challenge yourself and honestly determine if you can see the link from past to present.

Next, write down and answer these questions:

- How do I want to feel or behave about this right now?
- How do I want to feel or behave if it happens again?

Visualize yourself having a different feeling or behavior. Close your eyes for about a minute and walk yourself through the situation all over again, but this time be in control of your feelings and create the feeling you would have wanted to experience. See it all happening again, only this time with the new mental map that you are creating. When you do this visualization, use your five senses as you did when you were reliving your memories during step 2.

Next, write down and ask yourself, "What do I need to do right now as a result of my new truth?"

Perhaps you need to do something that will make up for an incident that happened that day. It could be an apology to a spouse or a child ("Sorry I overreacted today"). It could be an honest feeling statement to your spouse or child that you previously held back from saying ("I wanted to say I love you, but didn't" or "I felt hurt by what you did and didn't tell you"). Maybe there is something you need to do that you now realize you would have done if your own truth had been guiding you: eating a healthy meal, exercising, taking a relaxing bath, or making a phone call on your child's behalf.

Finally, consider the following and write it down: "My new truth is_____."

You've heard the expression that hindsight is twenty-twenty. It's easier (not necessarily *easy*) to see how you should've acted. Now I want you to believe that your foresight is twenty-twenty. Think about tomorrow and what is coming up for you. What is likely to happen, and how can you prepare your mental map to meet the challenge of not slipping into the old autopilot? Write a line or two about what you can change about tomorrow. Then say it aloud while looking in the mirror. Look specifically at this line when developing your new mission statement the next day.

Your Mission to Change

To achieve this step, the pages of your journal should contain the following for each new day:

1. Write a general mission statement.

2. Ask yourself specifically, "How will I best make this happen?"

3. Have two emotional checkups, one at midday and one at the end of the day. In this process you will address the following:

   Did I need to feel or behave the way I did?

   Would I have wanted to feel or behave differently?

   How do I wish I would have felt or behaved differently?

   What feelings or issues from my past would have possibly motivated me to feel or behave the way I did?

   How do I want to feel or behave about this right now?

   How do I want to feel or behave if it happens again?

4. At the end of your day, ask yourself, "What do I need to do right now as a result of my new truth?"

5. Write down your new truth and say it aloud in front of a mirror.

Now I'd like to take you back to both Sarah and Tim to show you how they came to change. The sections below are verbatim excerpts from their journals.

Sarah's Steps to Change

Just to remind myself:

Things I Most Want to Change
Low self-confidence and self-worth
Loneliness

Instability and a sense of feeling lost

Relationship issues

Trust issues

Sadness and anxiety

Trouble communicating

Can't handle confrontation

Sense of feeling numb

Anger, fighting

Before I did this [exercise] I tried to figure out which item on the list I wanted to start with. I do know they will all sort of interconnect at times, so the first thing I decided I needed to do is try to unisolate myself. The last nine months have been a perfect storm. I have recently isolated myself from all of the people around me: coworkers, friends, and family. I already keep people at arm's length, but usually I go to work every day and see people, and there's a lot of people interaction in my job and at work (I'm a pediatric physical therapist).

Last year I hurt my shoulder at work and have since been relegated to computer work, which means I'm usually all alone in an office while everyone is treating patients. I think I could probably get through most of my days without saying more than ten words to anyone at this point. And while I will still go out with my friends or family, my day-to-day [routine] is pretty much just me.

A lot of the items on that list require some form of interaction with other people. So first things first. I have to start by changing or increasing my interactions with the rest of the world.

Day 1

Mission Statement or Daily Goal (I'm expanding this title because I feel empowered by the words.)

General: To reconnect with old friends I haven't talked to in a while.

Specific (how will I best make this happen): I will call them and have at least a ten-minute conversation with two people.

Sarah's Emotional Checkup #1: Noon

I will be calling people after I get home from work. In some ways it'll be nice to find out what they're up to, but I also have some hesitation because I always wonder if they really want to talk to me. This is probably ridiculous, because I've been friends with the people I'm going to call since I was six years old.

Did I need to feel or behave the way I did? No, I probably don't need to feel like that.

Would I have wanted to feel or behave differently? I would rather just feel excited to know I'm going to talk to them.

How do I wish I would have felt or behaved differently? I wish I would have been excited by the opportunity and just been relaxed about the idea.

What feelings or issues from my past would have possibly motivated me to feel or behave the way I did? I guess since my parents didn't have that much interest in me, I just expect everyone else not to, either. Or that I'm not really sure why people would want to bother talking to me.

How do I want to feel or behave about this right now? If it happens again? Just content that I will get to talk to them *without* feeling like I'm not worth talking to.

What do I need to do right now as a result of my new truth? Press on.

My new truth is: I am interesting enough for people to want to be with me and spend time with me.

Sarah's Emotional Checkup #2: Mission Accomplished

Both phone calls made. One call took twenty minutes, and the other call was sixty minutes. Both friends seemed happy that I called. I probably listened more than I talked. I still had the same feelings initially that I had earlier in the day, but I felt better about those things after I got off the phone.

Did I need to feel or behave the way I did? No. I guess the fact that they have caller ID and still picked up the phone when they saw it was me should help convince me that they wanted to talk to me. But I have to admit I kept thinking before the phone calls that if they wanted to talk to me, then they could call me also. This thought led me to think they were only talking to me because they were forced, that they just sort of went along with it because I called.

Would I have wanted to feel or behave differently? Yes.

How do I wish I would have felt or behaved differently? I wish I just would have felt that they really did want to speak to me honestly and wholeheartedly.

What feelings or issues from my past would have possibly motivated me to feel or behave the way I did? Besides what I already wrote above, possibly the fact that I'm still kind of freaked out at the thought of getting close to someone, so maybe I'm just making up reasons to keep myself isolated.

How do I want to feel or behave about this right now? If it happens again? I want to feel like I know they want to talk to me and not that they're talking to me just to put up with me or just because I called and they have nothing better to do.

What do I need to do right now as a result of my new truth? Um, figure out who I'm going to call tomorrow?

My new truth is: That I can call my friends and know that they will want to talk to me. (And did you know how hard it is to say things to yourself in the mirror? Because I just found out, and it's *hard*.)

Day 2

Mission Statement or Daily Goal

General: To reconnect with coworkers face-to-face during lunch without feeling like they are just putting up with me, and to feel like they might want to talk to me. Also to reconnect with friends and feel like they would want to talk to me.

Specific: I will not do work during lunch. I will eat with my coworkers and talk to them. I will also call two more friends and talk to them for at least twenty minutes without feeling like they would not want to talk to me.

Sarah's Emotional Checkup #1: 11 a.m.

Pretty much I spent the morning talking to myself to sort of try to get excited about lunch instead of feeling kind of defeated. Last week I wasn't concerned about lunch before lunchtime, but I kind of was today. Did I need to feel that way? No. I would rather have just felt comfortable and confident and not concerned.

Sarah's Emotional Checkup #2: Wow, It Worked!

I was sitting in the office working before lunch. I had pulled out my lunch bag and it was on my desk. I was finishing one last thing before I went to lunch when my coworker Jane walked in. She asked me if I was done, and I finished what I was doing. I assumed that she needed to look up her schedule or something on the computer, but instead she actually turned the computer off, grabbed my lunch and said, "You're not eating alone in here while you do homework today. If you want your lunch, you'll just have to come and sit in the lunchroom."

She then walked out with my lunch. She called over her shoulder that I had five minutes to get in there before she ate my yogurt. Of course, I followed her to the lunch table, but I was more than a little surprised that she did that.

Did I need to feel or behave the way I did? I'm not sure. I think it should have made me happy or something like that. It more just made me confused, I think. I'm not sure exactly. So did I need to feel that way? Probably didn't need to feel confused or whatever it was I was feeling.

How do I wish I would have felt or behaved differently? I think I would have wanted this to make me happy.

What feelings or issues from my past would have possibly motivated me to feel or behave the way I did? I think that probably it would mostly be that no one really seemed to want me around at home, so I still just apply that to all situations.

How do I want to feel or behave about this right now? If it happens again? For starters, I'd just like to know for sure what I'm feeling! But how about happy or even just relieved that besides [my] not being rejected, someone actually sought me out!

What do I need to do right now as a result of my new truth? Throw myself into more of these situations to reaffirm the reality that I'm not unwanted and not everyone will reject me.

My new truth is: No matter how confused I am, I am likable and people want to be around me!

Sarah's Emotional Checkup #3: Reconnecting

Phone call to friends: Okay, only one of the two happened. The first phone call lasted way longer than I thought it would (two hours), so it was kind of late by the time I would have made my second phone call. It was bordering on too late to call, so I only did the one.

The call went fine. It was another friend I hadn't spoken to in a while. I think I kind of realized that this first round of calls might not be the hard ones and that the hard stuff might be the ones where I have to call often to really develop the relationship. I have now started worrying about that, even though I haven't even made it through my list of people to call yet.

Anyway, the one phone call was fine. I still felt a little anxious or uneasy before I did it, but nothing bad happened!

Did I need to feel or behave the way I did? No, I did not need to feel anxious or uneasy. Plus, I most certainly did not need to worry about the next round of calls when I'm not even done with these.

Would I have wanted to feel or behave differently? Yes.

How do I wish I would have felt or behaved differently? I wish that I could just do these things that everyone else does so easily without the worry and feeling anxious or uneasy. I would just like the absence of these feelings that seem to serve no purpose!

What feelings or issues from my past would have possibly motivated me to feel or behave the way I did? (1) Since my parents didn't have that much interest in me, I just expect everyone else not to, either. (2) I'm not really sure why people would want to bother talking to me. (3) I'm still kind of freaked out at the thought of getting close to someone, so maybe I'm just making up reasons to keep me isolated. (4) Fear of rejection.

How do I want to feel or behave about this right now? If it happens again? Just content and accepting that someone would want to talk to me and catch up with me. Not so disbelieving.

What do I need to do right now as a result of my new truth? Try to figure out if there are other ways I can sort of unisolate myself.

My new truth is: That my friends do want to talk and catch up with me in person, at work, and over the phone. That I don't really need to be so uneasy in those situations because nothing bad has happened yet. No one has gone away because I've called them or seen them at lunch.

Day 3

Mission Statement or Daily Goal

General: To continue to work on reconnecting with people and to do it without being concerned. To reconnect and be totally relaxed.

Specific: Going to lunch with my work group.

Sarah's Emotional Checkup #1: Getting More at Ease

So lunch is much better. Part of it might be that I'm finally getting sort of back into the swing of things on the days I'm there [at work]. I was able to just hang out and be more relaxed. I am definitely still cautious and think about what I would say before I ever say it, which is probably overkill for lunch with your coworkers. But overall I was more relaxed, and I didn't worry about lunch before it happened. It was all of a sudden just time for lunch. So that's good. I probably do not still have to be so cautious with what I say to my coworkers during a random lunchtime conversation. Overall I'd say this was the least stressful one yet.

Did I need to feel or behave the way I did? Yes! Really, I think I did well.

Would I have wanted to feel or behave differently? Slightly.

How do I wish I would have felt or behaved differently? I would like to get to the point where I'm not as cautious and always concerned about how people might use what I say against me.

What feelings or issues from my past would have possibly motivated me to feel or behave the way I did? No matter what I said or did, they really didn't want to spend any time with me. I'd feel so lonely and sad.

How do I want to feel or behave about this right now? If it happens again? I really think this is linked to the fact that I never knew at home if what I said would get someone mad at either me or the other parent. And I would never know when the next "attack" might come out of the blue. So I kind of treat everything like a potential attack.

What do I need to do right now as a result of my new truth? I'm beginning to realize now that my past has greatly influenced this (as I mentioned above). Lunch with your coworkers should be a pretty low threat, so it's probably time to knock that off.

My new truth is: I no longer have to worry about whether people want to be around me. The anxiety is over.

Sarah's Emotional Checkup #2: A Bold Move

This one is not exactly related to my mission statement or goal but should probably be written down because it's going to need to be one at some point. Long story short, I had something that I needed to tell my manager at work. She's fairly nice as long as you agree with her. If you don't agree with her, she tends to get all passive-aggressive and corporate talking. This was a time I did not agree with her. Confronting people is not my strong suit.

However, I've learned that if she is the one to initiate the meeting, I can go in there and sort of do okay. But if it's something where I have to be the one to initiate the conversation, I'm never able to do that. I can sort of do it over e-mail to some extent, but even then it's hard.

So here I had a situation where I knew I just needed to go in and say what I needed to say, and I could not. I seriously debated with myself for two hours. I'd tell myself "just go" and then I'd talk myself out of it. Or else it was like I was frozen. I ended up sending her an e-mail instead of talking to her about it.

Did I need to feel or behave the way I did? Two words: epic failure. It's not like I haven't had this conversation with myself before—but I'm still frozen? I mean, people do this all the time, yet I can't. Grrr. I feel kind of really ticked off at myself. So did I need to feel like I could not do this and then behave in [the sense] that I didn't do it? No, because people do this kind of thing every day—just not me.

Would I have wanted to feel or behave differently? Yes.

How do I wish I would have felt or behaved differently? I would want to feel like I could do this and have the ability to do this and not feel like it's something that's so scary that I just can't do it. Like I could just go up to someone and tell them something that maybe they don't want to hear. Okay, maybe starting with my boss is not the best idea—maybe someone more lateral to me, but still.

What feelings or issues from my past would have possibly motivated me to feel or behave the way I did? Let's see: I don't like fighting because it is scary and awful. And I have never seen an actual constructive confrontation—my parents only attacked to be mean and awful. And I can guarantee, even if I thought something was unfair and I would want to speak up about it, that I never, ever felt like I could because I didn't really get a say in anything, so what was the point? I'm also kind of scared at how I might act. Like if the conversation gets at all heated, like I could have one of my times where I just explode. It doesn't happen very often, but it always catches me by surprise. And it would be very bad if that happened while talking to my boss.

How do I want to feel or behave about this right now? If it happens again? I want to feel like I could do this and that everything would turn out okay. Like I'm capable of doing this thing that everyone else on the planet seems to have no problem doing. But I feel like I am so far away from that.

A random thought I just had is that maybe learning to confront people is worse than being numb and isolated and alone. Hmm—sounds like the obstacle "It's my normal. I don't know anything different."

What do I need to do right now as a result of my new truth? I'd like to figure out something that I could do that is between confronting my boss and being a spineless wimp. I don't think starting with my boss is a good idea. I probably have to start with someone who doesn't have the power to fire me. I'm not sure who that person is yet or what's in the middle of being a spineless wimp and confronting someone like a normal person. Gotta think about that.

My new truth is: Man, this day's truth is complicated. Okay, I'll start with the good part: I am much better able to reconnect with people from work and talk to them with much less stress, and I think this will continue to get better.

Okay, now the harder part: My next one should be that my coworkers do want to see me and are happy when I'm there. Furthermore, this should make me feel good. Okay, the next one should be that I'm able to confront people and say my point of view without thinking that I don't deserve my own point of view or that they will not listen to what I have to say. Also that I can say my views without destroying the relationship.

Day 4

Mission Statement or Daily Goal

General: At a wedding weekend today in my hometown. I am going to socialize and talk to people I know well and those I don't know well, and I'm going to celebrate the day for the great occasion it is and have fun!

Specific: No freaking out or stressing out about talking to people I'm not specifically close to.

Sarah's Emotional Checkup #1: Confidence Found

I went to a wedding in my hometown for a girl I used to babysit for who lived across the street from me. I've known her since she was born. When I was in college, her mom died and I started to be a nanny for them and became kind of like a surrogate mom to her. I can say that living with my dad for all those years made me much better able to help the children (two girls) who were now living alone with their dad.

Back to the wedding: I was nervous also because it was in my hometown, so I had to drive there, and some of my cousins were going to be at the wedding. I did a pretty good job of not worrying about today, though. I went to the pool at the hotel where the other people who were going to the wedding were staying and it was a relaxing day all around. Then again, we were all chilling out, reading books, swimming, etc., so it wasn't super social. But surprisingly I also was not worried about later this evening, either. So this is exactly how I would want to feel.

Sarah's Emotional Checkup #2: Working Hard at It

Okay, I did a pretty good job at the wedding and reception. Such a great thing to be able to witness, and it was nice to be around people who felt the same way. The reception went well but was definitely a challenge.

I was fine with the mingling before we sat down, because I could control who I talked to, so I stuck with the people I knew well. For dinner, I was at the table with the cousins I kind of know but do not know well, by any means. Plus, I didn't bring anyone with me as a guest, so it was just me and the cousins and their spouses. It was fine, but I felt like it was a lot of work. I don't exactly know how I felt. It wasn't exactly like I was worried, more like I just had to keep reminding myself to actually take part in the conversations.

Normally I would have just sat and listened without saying a word, unless asked a direct question. Now most of my effort was expended into actually forcing myself to have a conversation. It was almost like my attention was so directed on this that I didn't have time to be concerned or uneasy. I mean, it wasn't the most comfortable, stress-free night, so I must have had some uneasiness. It was more like I could either attend to doing the task or attend to how I was feeling, and I decided to more attend to doing the task at hand.

Did I need to feel or behave the way I did? Well, I wasn't super-worried or stressed out, so I think that was good. But I'm also not sure about not being able to attend to doing something and knowing how I feel about it. This kind of seems like my usual mode of operation: do what I need to do to get by, but just don't feel anything. The fact that I had to work so hard at it probably means something.

Would I have wanted to feel or behave differently? If I'm doing what I normally do, then yes. If I really was less stressed out, then no. But, really, I probably did well in the end, because I was not anxious.

How do I wish I would have felt or behaved differently? I want to be able to just not have to work so hard at things that seem so easy for everyone else! I want to actually just be at ease and not doubt myself. I don't want to feel that talking to someone wouldn't go well.

However, the fact is that overall the reception and dinner went fine, and that I was not constantly worried is great.

What feelings or issues from my past would have possibly motivated me to feel or behave the way I did? Still working on believing people would even want to have a conversation with me and that they won't use what I say against me. I think that is why this requires so much effort from me. I evaluate every little thing that comes out of my mouth because I'm constantly wondering how it could be used against me now or in the future.

How do I want to feel or behave about this right now? If it happens again? Calm and to not have to work so hard at it.

What do I need to do right now as a result of my new truth? Really understand what I've written and put it into practice—things I say won't be used against me and I have to keep putting myself into these situations to reaffirm that belief so it becomes my new truth.

My new truth is: I *can* talk to people without anything bad happening.

Day 5

Mission Statement or Daily Goal

General: To make it through the day and, most important, dinner tonight with my dad and stepmom without snapping at or yelling at anyone. Why? Because I am mad and ticked off at everyone! I don't know who I'm mad at or exactly why. Grrr—I finally begin feeling something, and this is the feeling that pops out. Swell.

Specific: This is kind of the opposite of what I've been trying to do overall, but I think my best bet is to engage as little as possible. This is going to be tricky. My emergency backup plan would be to just shut down, but I'm really trying not to do that.

Sarah's Emotional Checkup #1: Trepidation Overcome

Still at the wedding weekend. Had coffee with my cousin and her daughter this morning. My cousin loves to talk about herself nonstop, so I just let her. Lots of nodding and agreeing. Plus, hung out with her two-year-old daughter, which helped because I am not nearly as ticked off when hanging out with an adorable little girl. My cousin has not done anything to make me mad, so I wish that I could have just enjoyed seeing her, instead of working hard not to say something snippy or act mad. I would have wanted to be able to separate my cousin from my feeling mad, because it probably has nothing to do with her, and so it shouldn't have had to affect our time together.

Sarah's Emotional Checkup #2: My Aunt Made Me Angry

After bringing my cousin home, my aunt was there and I got sucked into going to lunch and the mall with her. This was more tricky than coffee, because my aunt is possibly the most self-absorbed, drama-loving person I know. If she wasn't my aunt, I would for sure have already phased her out of my life long ago. She is just seriously annoying and just sucks energy from people around her. She never has anything nice to say about anyone.

So while she bashed people during lunch, I got even madder because instead of saying something nasty to her, I just sat and smoldered and bit my tongue about a thousand times. I don't think my aunt had anything to do with my bad mood, but I also think that she didn't help it.

Sarah's Emotional Checkup #3: Indigestion Would Have Been Easier

Dinner at my dad's, with my dad, stepmother, and stepsister. If we weren't celebrating his birthday, I would have probably come up with some fake illness to get out of going. That is how much I did not want to go, mainly because already dealing with my mom this week has only served to increase my irritation at the world. I didn't think this dinner was going to help that, and I was right.

Watching my dad and stepmom sit and pretend that we're this little Beaver Cleaver fake family bothered me way more than usual. Only it usually makes me want to just make gagging noises, and today I wanted to strangle everyone!

So I hung out with my three-year-old stepnephew, who was much preferable company to everyone else. Then during dinner I chewed my food a lot and let them all talk to each other. After dinner was harder because I had nothing to keep my mouth busy. So I had to interact and totally pretend that I wasn't in a bad mood. Finally we played Liverpool rummy, so at least I got to pretend that I was just very involved in the game, even though I was more interested in finishing the game so I could go home.

I pretty much felt the same way the whole night—mad. And while they have not done anything to all of a sudden make me mad, being at home definitely made it more heightened.

Did I need to feel or behave the way I did? I don't even know why I feel this way right now. So I don't know!

Would I have wanted to feel or behave differently? Yes. I would rather not feel like this. But I did make it through the evening without turning all numb. So although it took all my willpower to not act like I was mad and ticked off at everyone, I was able to get through without my emergency backup option. So I guess that was good. Plus, at least I was feeling something.

How do I wish I would have felt or behaved differently? How about anything other than mad!

What feelings or issues from my past would have possibly motivated me to feel or behave the way I did? I just read this over, and it occurred to me that when I was a kid, the pretending in the family always made me feel so disconcerted and my stepmom always made me mad.

How do I want to feel or behave about this right now? If it happens again? (1) Try not to slip into being numb, which is kind of a fight because I am not a big fan of being mad at the world. (2) I need to figure out how to not be mad anymore, or maybe it would just be nice if I could figure out why I'm all of a sudden so ticked off and exactly who I could direct this toward. I'd prefer the first option, because the second option still leaves me possibly in a similar situation.

What do I need to do right now as a result of my new truth? I just read this over, and it seems my anger sort of escalated as I approached the evening with my dad. So what was probably making me mad is having to go to dinner at my dad's in the first place!

Maybe it was the anticipation of having to be in a place where everything is fake and I'm made to pretend. Lately I've been coming to a place of reality, and this reverting back to my childhood (dinner with my dad and the "perfect" family) just made me truly and deeply upset. So maybe it was good that I felt something. Normally I would have just ignored the feeling and pressed on, but looking at it, although I didn't like the feeling, is probably a step in the right direction. So maybe I was or am angry at my dad and his new family.

My new truth is: I can manage to feel something without reverting to being numb, and I also managed not to explode at anyone.

Tim's Steps to Change

Day 1

Mission Statement or Daily Goal

General: Today I want to accept things as they come and not get stressed-out or overwhelmed when or if they don't go "my way."

Specific: The best way to make this happen is to realize a lot of the things that stress me out are very minor. I need to reframe how I think about things.

Tim's Emotional Checkup #1: Worry, Worry

Feeling pretty good and getting work done. I am worrying about my son and his soccer tryouts this afternoon, worried about his performance in this hundred-degree-plus temperature. Not obsessing over it, though.

Tim's Emotional Checkup #2: Now I'm Obsessing!

Now I am really obsessing over my son's tryouts. My wife and I both were there, and it was *hot* outside and they ran the kids very hard. Halfway through, he told my wife he was *done*. He was cramping and overheated. I was all set to have him sit it out, but she encouraged him to stay, and he made it through and was so proud afterward. Now I'm very upset that he was so uncomfortable and that he almost quit. I know that if I had been the only one there with him, I would have let him walk away from a sport he loves just because of one hard tryout. That bothers me the most—I would have let him quit.

Did I need to feel or behave the way I did? No, I don't need to feel this way. He's almost thirteen years old and can handle a lot more than I think he can. Life does get uncomfortable at times, and I need to allow my kids to feel these things.

Would I have wanted to feel or behave differently? I would definitely like to feel differently and quit thinking about this. I need to know my kids are not me and they have the tools to handle situations that I did not have as a kid. They are much better adjusted and deserve to have experiences. Although I was afraid to do new things and never did, they are not the kid I was.

How do I wish I would have felt or behaved differently? I wish I wasn't obsessing over my son having a hard tryout and knowing I would've let him quit. Why do I obsess so much? I try to change things in my mind to make them better or different.

What feelings or issues from my past would have possibly motivated me to feel or behave the way I did? My past feelings that have motivated me to feel this way are that I hated awkward situations as a kid and very often felt out of control. I felt a lot of discomfort in new situations. I can't stand to think my kids will ever feel the same way I did, so I want to try to keep them from that.

How do I want to feel or behave about this right now? If it happens again? I want to accept that both of my children may not always be happy in a given situation, but I want to understand that my wife and I have given and can continue to give them the tools to deal with things. They will grow and mature and learn new things—even if they are uncomfortable at times.

What do I need to do right now as a result of my new truth? I need to let go of my worries as a result of my new truth. Let my kids fall at times and allow them to have the chance to flourish on their own.

My new truth is: Not everything is in my control, and that is okay. I can allow things to pan out as they will—even if it's not what I want. There is no way anyone can control every situation. I can control how I react, though.

Day 2

Mission Statement or Daily Goal

General: Today my wife and I have a lot to get done, with visitors coming for the weekend. I want it to be okay when everything is not perfect.

Specific: I want to get done what I can and accept what I can't.

Tim's Emotional Checkup #1: Copping Out

Too stressed; my wife is running around picking up things, and so I went to the grocery store early this morning and now I'm at work. Feeling rushed.

Tim's Emotional Checkup #2: Nasty Me

Overwhelmed and tired. Not happy that I wasn't pleasant at work; I glared at an inconsiderate coworker, and that really wasn't necessary. I was impatient with my wife, too. Disappointed that I couldn't be busy and pleasant at the same time.

Did I need to feel or behave the way I did? I did not need to behave or feel this way. It has always been my pattern to get irritable unless everything is calm and perfect.

Would I have wanted to feel or behave differently? I would like to behave differently.

How do I wish I would have felt or behaved differently? I would like to enjoy every day instead of becoming unhappy because I don't feel like everything is in line. I should know nothing is ever going to be perfect and sometimes you just have to roll with the punches.

What feelings or issues from my past would have possibly motivated me to feel or behave the way I did? I think the feelings from my past that motivated me to feel this are that I wanted everyone in my household to be content. However, that was rarely the case. My parents would be mad at each other, and my sister would be mad at my dad. I couldn't stand it—I felt very insecure because of the lack of peace. In my head, I just felt there had to be a way I could make it right. However, it didn't matter, I never made it right. As a result, I was pissed off most of the time. I would become difficult and irritable with my family.

How do I want to feel or behave about this right now? If it happens again? The next time I feel rushed and irritable, I want to take a deep breath and consider that most of these things are not that big of a deal. I want to realize that I'm not in control of events around me—no one is, and that's okay.

What do I need to do right now as a result of my new truth? I need take a step back and realize that my past circumstances are affecting the here and now. I need to understand that I'm no longer that little boy needing to keep my house and everyone in it from falling apart. I'm an adult, and my life now is okay and overall peaceful.

My new truth is: Things happen in the day that I can't control. I'm going to control my behavior and attitude and try to deal with things in a pleasant manner.

Day 3

Mission Statement or Daily Goal

General: I will try to not become overwhelmed today.

Specific: The best way to do this is to be prepared and to give myself enough credit to know I can do it.

Tim's Emotional Checkup #1: Getting All Ticked Off

My wife was coming back from out of town, and I had to pick up the kids from school and then go pick her up. The thing is, she said she didn't want me to pick her up. She said it was unnecessary for me to drive the two hours and that she'd just rent a car or have her friend pick her up. When I heard this, I got really upset. Why don't you want me to come pick you up? You don't want to see me? I even thought for a second maybe she doesn't love me.

Did I need to feel or behave the way I did? I felt anxious, and my heart started pounding. I got angry at her for a simple stupid thing.

Would I have wanted to feel or behave differently? Yes, I don't want to get upset over the small things.

How do I wish I would have felt or behaved differently? I wish I would have just been able to calmly see it from her perspective. She was trying to be nice! I had been holding down the fort for the last three days, and she knew I was tired, so she didn't want me to have to leave the kids and come all the way to get her, but I couldn't see that.

What feelings or issues from my past would have possibly moti-vated me to feel or behave the way I did? My mom left when I was young for a long time, and we had no idea when or even if she was coming back. I thought she didn't love me, because she didn't want to be around me. So I guess I extended that fear to my wife.

How do I want to feel or behave about this right now? If it hap-pens again? I want to see things from other people's perspectives. I want to look at the small situations in life without being influ-enced by my own automatic thoughts.

What do I need to do right now as a result of my new truth? If something bothers me, I need to stop before I respond. I need to remind myself that maybe I'm just having automatic thoughts that are unjustified for the situation.

My new truth is: There is no need to be afraid that people will leave without an explanation. I owe it to myself and to my family to trust and have faith in them.

Making the Shift

As we've followed Sarah and Tim, we've seen their intense struggles. At times they wondered if they were getting any-where, but they persevered and worked on change consis-tently, which allowed them to see life with their eyes wide open. They each had an epiphany and it stuck. However, it didn't happen overnight. It was a process of gradual growth as they continued to force themselves to confront their own issues and truth, which in turn allowed them to see a whole new way of living.

Change isn't going to happen overnight for you, either. So be like Sarah and Tim and take it a day at a time or even an hour at a time. You too will persevere. It is very common for people to think they're not doing a good enough job when they first start going through this process of change. Here are some examples of feelings expressed by other people early in the process:

"I should've done much better."
—Barbara

"My mission statement was not challenging enough."
—Peggy

"Seeing my attempts to change makes me feel so pathetic that I can't do better."
—Alan

"I can't believe at my age I need to be making mission statements daily. How pathetic."
—Debbie

"Why can't I just control myself!"
—Brian

"If it's this hard, it must mean it's not the right way for me to change."
—Carol

"I must've done something wrong in an earlier step, because this is not going like I had hoped."
—Sharon

"Who has the time for all this? I can't be this messed up."
—Nick

Do you hear yourself in any of these statements? They all come from a feeling of worthlessness. It's autopilot pulling them back to the direction of their mental maps. This happens. It's perhaps the most difficult part of the process, like a tug-of-war. You need to be cognizant of this happening in order to fight back and stay on course.

Shifting away from autopilot means there will be sunny days and rainy days. There are going to be many days where you realize you've been operating on autopilot, and you'll be unhappy that you didn't see it at the time so you could do something about it. The only thing you can do is be honest with yourself—"Oops, I slipped back"—and continue to persevere. Remind yourself, "Look how far I've come!"

If it gets you angry, that's okay. Anger can fuel your determination to keep working and finally begin to make real changes, as long as you don't get too down on yourself. Just don't get impatient.

Parental Warning

There is a delicate situation that bears warning: time with your parents. Since so many of your issues are tied to your childhood experiences, it is very common that your autopilot will be making its most powerful tug when you are around your parents. It's possible that watching their behavior, even just hearing your parents' voices, will send you right back to those negative feelings in a heartbeat. This can happen even if your parents do nothing offensive or hurtful. And it's almost certain to happen when a parent does something that you find hurtful or annoying.

This time of change is not a good time for spontaneous visits to or from your parents. Plan these events so you can prepare for them. This means putting some time in to consider how you used to feel around them and how you want to change when you are around them from now on. It's a unique challenge, but you can manage it well as long as you make the effort.

Talk Back to Your Autopilot

As you go through the process of change, you will quickly become aware of what a powerful force autopilot and your past can be. As hard as it fights you, you can fight it even harder.

If a change day doesn't go so well, realize that that's life. Don't allow the negative messages of childhood to make you feel hopeless. It's common for people going through change to get upset with themselves if a day doesn't turn out to be any different from the past. Getting upset with yourself because you're not progressing as you had hoped is yet another insidious way for your autopilot to get the best of you. Don't let it happen.

Be proud of yourself just for the work you've achieved. You've come a long way in freeing yourself from the negative buzz that comes from childhood. Give yourself a pat on the back every day, and keep forging on. You'll make it.

A Job Well Done

Do this exercise once you've completed the first two weeks of change.

Envision the issues of your past that you have been working to change. See yourself physically placing each one into a collective trash bag. Next, see yourself building a wall in front of it, cementing it in brick by brick. Build the wall as high as you can. When you are finished, step up close to the wall and feel its coolness. Push on it and feel its strength. Now push really hard and see it fall over onto the bag of stuff you tied up. Take a deep breath and watch yourself in your mind's eye walking away and applauding yourself for a job well done.

7

Going Forward

Maintaining the Healing

The formal program has ended, but this is really just the beginning—of a new you. You will need to stay with the change process for a few months, in order for it to stick, before you will be able to finally recognize true change in yourself. The only way to attain change is to build it little by little.

Do not beat yourself up if the change doesn't seem to be happening fast enough or if it starts to upset you. Consider it all as part of the pattern. You have to get to the point where you see the *need* for change so crystal clear that you can't close your eyes to it anymore. On days when you think you've made little progress, choose to embrace the progress you made and feel worthy so that you can gain the strength to make more changes tomorrow.

Realize that even when you have moments or days when change is difficult, the mere struggle is building mental muscle for you to be able to change tomorrow. It's like building your biceps. At first it's hard, and you're sore from the exercise. Many days you don't feel like exercising, but if you stick with it, in time it will be unmistakably real and a new part of you.

This is likely to be the hardest task of your life. Change is hard because it requires going deep within yourself. It is a constant, detailed analytical process, but once it takes hold, the struggle is gone. Your new outlook on life and your feelings about yourself will feel as natural to you as your past life did.

The process of getting there does not take forever. If you put yourself wholeheartedly into this process, within a relatively short time you will begin to see changes in your life. You'll notice that you're naturally acting differently without having to make the effort to do so. Eventually your healthier mindset will become your new normal, your new autopilot. This doesn't mean that you won't still find yourself sometimes behaving in a way that slips back to the old, unfortunate internal messages. But that will become the exception rather than the rule.

You will naturally believe yourself to be worthy and will live your life using your new belief system. This can take a while, surely at least four to six months. But you'll begin to see change the moment you truly learn how to focus. As the days and weeks pass, you will see yourself needing to think about the change less and less and will start to realize you are feeling it more and more.

In the meantime, and for the foreseeable future, concentrate intensely on your focus every day. Don't let up. In the last two weeks you were writing your daily mission statement and doing emotional checkups without a miss. It was certainly intense. You need to continue doing this. You can keep it as a daily ritual if that is working for you. However, you can also choose to let up a bit. For the next month, I recommend that you do your mission statement and emotional checkups three times a week. Then do it twice a week for another month. Thereafter, write a mission statement and do an emotional checkup once a week.

Make sure to follow through on all of the aspects of the mission statement that you learned in the final step. In the months ahead, train yourself to have a minimum of two emotional checkups daily, even if you don't write them down, until you feel confident you've changed your mental map. You must keep up your awareness for this to work. Remember how deeply you are digging to develop this ultimate change. It will come only with great awareness.

The emotional checkups are crucial. If you feel like you're slipping, start writing more daily mission statements and write down your emotional checkups as well.

Awareness Is Your Friend

Life has a tendency to overwhelm. Stress makes your guard go down and lets your autopilot settle in as comfortable as an old shoe. This is why you must always be aware of your feelings. Awareness is crucial. Never let your guard down, or else your old autopilot will jump right in and take over.

Reinforce your awareness by going back through your journal. Read it, review it, and reflect on your recent writings. This is especially important when life starts moving too fast.

There will also be times when the work required in this process feels like too much. You'll have wonderful, rational excuses to get away from it: It takes too much time. You're just too tired. You have so many other emotional issues going on that you can't deal with one more burden. You have company visiting and need to be at your best. Your dog needs extra love.

Whatever clever distraction you'd like to use, recognize clearly that this is nothing more than your autopilot working overtime to get back in as your primary source of living. It's getting nervous and freaking out.

Obviously, this old autopilot has been part of you for a long time and is the belief system you've come to accept. Consider it toxic. Just because this parasite has lived in you this long doesn't mean it deserves a free ride forever. Root it out and expel it by filling yourself with your new truth and how you choose to feel and behave.

It's so important that you understand how much mental energy change requires. But it will be so much less than all of the energy it took to keep yourself down and beholden to the messages of your childhood.

The Only Time to Stop the Program

This program calls for deep change and, as such, is a very serious tool. In order to work, it requires that you repeatedly push yourself mentally. As a result, people who have suffered from certain depressive disorders or have attempted suicide may find the program overwhelming.

This program is designed to help you gain confidence, feel emotionally stronger, and get in control of your life. This is why it moves you through certain sad stages quickly. If you find yourself becoming depressed and feeling unable to function in your life, stop the program and seek immediate medical or psychological attention. If you wish to continue with the program at a later point, talk to your doctor first or find a therapist to help you through it.

Your Maintenance Plan

Anyone who has lost weight knows that you have to have a maintenance plan to make the weight loss permanent. The same goes for this program. You can't swear off feelings any more than you can swear off food. This means you're always going to remember the old you even as you're aware how much you want to keep the new you. This program has shown you that there is a new way of living, and it consists of always growing.

Even after you have finished the program and you're feeling great about yourself many months from now, a situation might arise that challenges your confidence and self-esteem. You might start questioning yourself or get a feeling of being off track. When this happens, pull out your journal and revisit the process. Review your work and the messages you've written to yourself.

There may come a time when you'll want to redo the program completely. For example, perhaps you helped yourself feel worthy and changed the way you relate to your spouse and your kids. But two years down the line you find yourself gaining weight and not taking care of your physical self in general. Consider starting the process all over again, focusing on taking care of yourself. Don't just focus on your weight and physical health from your childhood, although you should start there. Remember how you *feel* when you aren't taking care of yourself. What messages are you sending yourself at that moment? Take those feelings and consider them as they relate to your childhood.

We change in stages. We often have to repeat a process many times, and each time we are able to dig deeper. It would be nice to say we're healed, but no one who is committed to growing ever says that. We always want to get better at life and choose how to live it. So don't ever feel disappointed if you feel a need to get into the program mode again. If you feel disappointed, that just means your old autopilot is trying to get the better of you. Whenever you think you've strayed too far from awareness, go back to the program and review it or start all over. You'll be shocked at how much clearer things seem to get each time.

Did you ever see a movie you love multiple times? Each time you watch it you see something different, something you didn't catch before because you were too focused on the general message or the picture. It's the same for the movie of your own life. As you revisit the process each time, you can search for smaller details you weren't able to focus on previously. Each time, going through the process will bring you new details and nuances that will make your "life movie" richer.

Your Future with Change

Follow this schedule for journal writing and recording your mission statements:

Two weeks: Every day

One month: Three times weekly

Second month: Twice weekly

Third through fifth months: Once a week

In addition, continue to do a minimum of two emotional checkups daily, even if you don't write them down.

You are never done growing and understanding yourself, and re-righting will always be a great way to help you refocus. Find your own maintenance plan and make sure you stick with it.

There is always something healthy about stopping yourself and seeing how you are doing emotionally. My suggestion is that you have two emotional checkups daily for the next year. Write in your journal once to twice a week and keep it close by so that you can jot things down whenever something insightful hits you.

You lose nothing and only gain by creating a daily lifestyle in which you check up on yourself and focus on living your day as you wish to live it, without slipping back into the unfortunate personal beliefs of the past. The more energy you put into continuing with change, the more positive the change you invite into your life will be. It's your decision. It's your life. Choose to live it in a way that makes you feel worthy.

PART 3

Resolving Major Issues

8

Finding Peace with Your Parents Today

There is a lot of love lost as a result of divorce, and I'm not talking about between Mom and Dad. My research found that only 68 percent of adults who were children of divorce reported having a positive relationship with their mothers, and even less, 46 percent, said the same about their fathers.

This means that most of you have been left with a feeling of isolation from at least one parent and very often from both parents. It is the ongoing dream of the children of divorce that their parents will finally understand and love them the way they've always hoped to be loved. Now that you're an adult, you might have a relationship with a parent that is still strained. It would not be uncommon for you to still harbor resentment and hurt left over from childhood.

TRACY'S STORY
"I Lost My Daddy"

Here is a very common story. Perhaps it will resonate with your own feelings. The following section is Tracy's own words.

I remember the day my father told me he was moving in with his new girlfriend. I was seven, and all I wanted was my daddy. Was that wrong? I used to think it was, but I've come to see that any little girl would want her father. But he chose her over me. Once he moved in with her, suddenly he lived too far away for me to come visit. No more overnights, except a week or two in the summer. Instead I was reduced to a dinner here and there and a Saturday movie or visit to the mall.

When I was fifteen, I told him I didn't want to see him anymore. He seemed sad, but didn't do much about it. At my college graduation, I asked him why he left me. Can you believe that I'm dealing with this at my graduation? But I hadn't seen him for a few years. He told me he was sorry, but he couldn't take my mom and would've gone crazy if he had had to deal with her. He explained that even if it meant giving me up, he'd decided he would. He apologized, and all I thought was "If she was so awful for you, what about [for] me? Did you think that leaving me [with her] was just fine and dandy?"

We have continued to have a relationship since he divorced his second wife, but I hate him for this. I can barely get through a holiday dinner. I wish he could just listen and understand me. I don't want him to even apologize, just understand what it really felt like for me. I just want to tell him, but I know he'll just defend himself and never understand.

....

Getting to Forgiveness

How to forgive your parents, the people you love who have hurt you, is on the mind of every child of divorce. Forgiveness is often bandied about like a magic potion—once you forgive, it's done and that's that. It's not so easy.

Forgiveness is often asked and granted without great thought or emotional understanding. Saying "I'm sorry" can be almost as perfunctory as asking "How are you?" With deeply painful issues, many people feel such pressure to forgive that they rush to it without really achieving any peace internally. It is true that forgiving can be cleansing and calming, but too often it isn't, because it hasn't been dealt with in a manner that truly helps the one who was offended to be at peace.

Know What You Are Truly Looking For

The first question to ask yourself is whether an apology is really what you're after. An apology can actually lead to more pain, depending on the way it is made. Someone can say, "I'm sorry," but it may not be satisfactory because it didn't seem to come with much understanding.

Ideally, the apology should verbalize your parent's understanding of what his or her actions or inactions did to you. Saying "I'm sorry" has little healing effect unless there is some genuine discussion about how the behavior has hurt you. It's almost always crucial for you to be given a chance to describe to your parent what it was like for you to be hurt by the behavior. If this happens, you may be willing to forgive and even forget because you believe your parent now understands the effect these actions had on you. A heartfelt apology, together with the knowledge that you are more in control today, will significantly reduce the odds of you being hurt again.

Proceed Cautiously

If you have lived through your parent's behavior and have experienced the pain time and again, you should be wary. Chances are this person is capable of hurting you again in the future. An apology will therefore not accomplish anything. Unless your parent offers you firm reasoning and planning— therapy or more conversation with you—about why you won't be hurt in the future, you should probably expect similar hurtful behavior in the future. Deal with reality, not the fantasy of what you want.

Forgiving Yourself

As part of your healing journey, forgiveness of your parents can help. But the true issue is forgiving yourself. When you are hurt as a child, you carry pain that comes from a belief that in some way this hurt was deserved, that somehow your parents were responding to how unlovable you were. By the time you are an adult and figure out that it was only a result of your parents' personal issues, it's too late. Healing the pain within is what allows you to forgive others, because you realize that people hurt others because they had their own issues. Remember that their issues drove their ugly behavior; it is no reflection on you.

Forgive yourself today. Write yourself a long apology for thinking so poorly of yourself all of these years. Make it clear to yourself why you made this mistake. You may be repeating some of the work you did during the program, but it's worth it because this is focused solely on forgiveness.

Forgiveness is the culmination of loving yourself and knowing that no matter how far you have veered from being good to yourself, you can always confront, correct, and give yourself the gift of a genuine life that is yours to lead.

Are You Ready to Take This Step?

Wouldn't it be wonderful to finally hear a genuine apology from your parents for the wrongs of the past? Wouldn't it make such a difference in your relationship to hear them just acknowledge your feelings?

I have helped many adults meet with their parents and create a closer relationship by openly and safely discussing the past. A few years ago, on *The Oprah Winfrey Show*, I helped various adults have a conversation about their feelings and continued hurt with their divorced parents. It was very moving. The question is whether this is something you should now consider.

In deciding, there is one key element to determine: What is your goal?

Avoid the Wrong Approach

You need to carefully consider discussing your feelings with your parents; most of these conversations fail miserably because there is not much planning ahead of time. It's important that you understand going in what you want to accomplish.

There are realistic and unrealistic expectations involved in the process of finally getting your feelings off your chest. More often than not, our instincts and emotions cause us to take the wrong approach.

If you are really angry and might end up in a screaming match or just venting the ills of your past, what's the point? Is that what you want? I doubt it. You're entitled to express yourself as you desire, but are you going to feel better? It's more likely you'll feel guilty for unloading and regret having had the conversation in the first place. When meetings turn to venting, nothing gets accomplished—other than everyone knowing that there's intense anger and that there's now going to be tension every time you're all together in the future.

Is your goal to have your parent tell you something that will change your life or heal you? This is a dangerous goal because it is unrealistic and places too much control back in your parent's hands. You do not want to regress to where you are once again feeling emotionally dependent on your parent. It's also unrealistic to expect this from your parent, because his or her past actions suggest a personality that is not likely to express the loving and warm response you're hoping to get. You feel failed by this parent, and it is unlikely that one conversation will undo all of your past hurt.

Is your goal to blame your parent and make him or her feel bad for the pain you were caused? Even if you believe you could do this without the conversation ending up in a heated argument, which it almost definitely will, you won't feel any better.

As I've stressed from the start of this book, blame doesn't achieve anything. It's only a reminder that your autopilot is still trying to control you. There is little reason to go in any of these directions if you want to take control of your life. All you'll be doing is spewing hurt back at your parent, which accomplishes nothing.

There's Risk in Seeking the Truth

There is another entirely different reason for wanting to meet with your parents that is also dangerous, but I understand if you still want to give it a try: wanting the truth. Like many adults who were children of divorce, you may believe that your parents were dishonest with you, and it hurt you deeply. You have the urge to revisit these issues as an adult and finally get the honesty that was stolen from you as a child.

The problem is that once again you're putting a great deal of control into the hands of the parent who was dishonest with you in the first place. So think about it logically. You now want to demand the truth from someone who, for whatever reason—sometimes a quite understandable one—decided to lie to you. There is no rationale for you to assume that the reason for the lie has changed. Assuming that the parent will now properly represent the past with honesty and clarity is a stretch, don't you think? The chances are that it is not going to happen.

It's possible that you have a parent you trust and believe is basically honest and sincere. Perhaps Mom didn't want to tell you that Dad was cheating on her. Maybe Dad didn't want to tell you negative things about Mom. But even if your parent is willing to be honest with you now, do you really want to know? Will it really help you, or will it just confirm how screwed up your family's life was and how much pain it caused you? Also keep in mind that any question you ask will most likely be answered from a subjective point of view. After all, it's hard for anyone to be completely objective about his or her marriage, let alone one that ended more than twenty years ago.

You have to decide what you want to achieve when confronting your parent about the lies you were told. If you believe you were lied to, then you can surely get together with your parent to tell him or her just that. But trying to force the truth out of your parent and then assume you'll believe it this time just isn't a healthy approach.

Before you take this risky step, think about it carefully. Perhaps a better way to try to release this pain is through re-righting.

The Right Goal: Being Heard

The best way to have a conversation about the hurt of your childhood is to approach your parents with the goal of being heard. It's the most you can realistically hope for, but it's a goal that can be immensely satisfying. You want one moment in time when your parent actually listens and begins to feel what it was like to be you as a child.

You might think that you have never been able to articulate this well, or perhaps you have been too angry to do so. Now, as a result of going through this program, you're feeling more healed and in control of your life. You are now prepared to connect with your parents in a more honest way—but only if you so desire.

This is a goal worth seriously considering. You're not looking for an apology. This goal doesn't demand that your parent create some deep, meaningful response. If your parent really understands you, he or she may choose to apologize, but you can't begin a conversation expecting that.

The benefit of this type of meeting comes simply from being *heard*. It can foster your healing process to know that once and for all you've connected with your parent and helped the little kid inside you to express what was never properly heard years ago.

Another positive goal is to identify ways that you and your parent can become closer, again assuming this is something you want. This kind of discussion will give you an opportunity to continue to create healthy dialogue in the future.

Fair Warning

In some cases a parent just isn't going to listen, no matter what. If you've been getting this message, take it as a fair warning and remember that it is not a reflection on you.

You may not be able to accomplish anything if your parent is mean-spirited or has clearly expressed an unwillingness to get into any type of serious conversation about your past. Maybe your parent is highly defensive and unwilling to take any responsibility.

Maybe you've written a letter about how you feel and either never received a response or received a disappointing one. Maybe you've already had a disappointing, demoralizing conversation. Ask yourself whether trying to talk again is going to be any different. If so, does the conversation stand a good chance of having a positive outcome? If you think your parent is likely to listen and understand you, it's worth a try.

It's also important to keep in mind that having a conversation with a parent about your hurtful childhood is not in itself going to be healing, but it can help you to move along your path to healing. So if your parent doesn't respond in a sympathetic way, remember that you didn't lose much. You'll feel disappointed, but as long as you don't have much riding on the conversation, it is not going to cause more hurt. That's why it's crucial to know the reason you're having this conversation and how you need to plan to go about it.

The Dos and Don'ts of Confrontation

If you want to have a meaningful discussion with one or both of your parents about the effect of their divorce on your childhood, carefully consider your goal.

The following goals are dangerous because they are likely to add to your hurt:

Venting about how your parent messed up your childhood

Blaming your parents for the hurt they've caused you

Seeking an apology for the wrongs your parents committed in the past

> Using conversation as a means to feel healed

The following goals are positive and good reasons to open a discussion:

> To finally be heard

> To strengthen your relationship with your parents

> To facilitate the healing process

> To talk about practical ways to make the relationship better in the future

How to Accomplish Your Goal

Once you're clear about your goal, you need to carefully consider how to accomplish it.

1. Tell Your Parent You Want to Talk about Something Serious

It's unfair to sneak this conversation in as though it just happened to come up while you were home for the holidays, for example. If you want to get the best response from your parent, let him or her know you want to have a conversation about something important to you. Express your need for undivided attention and privacy.

Spontaneity is never a good idea. Sometimes people think that casually starting a conversation is a good idea because it won't look like such a big deal and it will create an easier flow of conversation. This is never the case. Instead, it usually results in a gross misunderstanding on the part of the parent, who doesn't realize its importance and, as a result, doesn't give it the respect it deserves.

Let your parent know what you need as a prelude to the conversation. Consider something like this:

> I have something serious I need to talk to you about. It involves my past and some of my issues, and I would like

about half an hour of your time when you and I can be alone, undisturbed, and uninterrupted, so we can talk. It's important to me to have this time, so please let me know when you can find the time to make this happen.

2. Set Up an Appropriate Time and Place

Just because your parent says that he or she can have the conversation right now, even though the grandchildren are running around the house and Thanksgiving dinner will soon be ready, that doesn't mean you have to concur. You don't want to feel rushed, hungry, or tired while having this conversation. You also don't want to have it over alcoholic drinks. You want your parent be clearheaded and fresh as well, although you don't have much control over this.

One of the biggest mistakes is giving in to ridiculous circumstances out of concern that if the conversation doesn't happen now, it will never happen. If your parent can't (or won't) find the proper time to have this conversation, it's best not to have it at all.

You also need a time limit. Keep the conversation to thirty minutes, then bring it to a close. If you spend more time talking, the conversation is likely to meander, and that can lead to other touchy topics that aren't related to your goal. Set the conversation up for success.

3. Take Control of the Conversation

You made the request, so you should be running the show. If you like, be prepared with written notes on the points you want to make. You want this conversation to be heartfelt, but you also don't want to walk away feeling you forgot to say something important. Begin the conversation yourself so that it's clear that you have an agenda and a purpose for getting together.

4. Set the Agenda on What You Want from Your Parent

When you request the meeting, your parent will probably be unsure of what it is you want to talk about. Start off the meeting by making your agenda known. Consider something like this:

> Dad, I have some difficult things to share, and I want you to listen. It may make you feel bad, but please understand that I'm not looking for you to do anything about it right now. I'm not looking for an apology. That'll be up to you, but you don't have to apologize. I don't want you to even speak at all until I'm completely finished with what I have to say. All I want is that you listen to me carefully and know that I want you to understand how I feel. I'm not looking to make you feel bad. I'm not looking to turn this into anything about you. It would just be so meaningful and such a gift from you if for this moment you can really hear what I'm sharing so that I feel you truly understand.

Clarify what you want and don't want from your parent during this meeting.

5. Stay on Task and Don't Stray

If you're feeling good about the conversation, there's a tendency to begin sharing things that you had never intended to discuss now. There's danger in this, because you'll move away from your original agenda and get onto a topic for which the conversation may not go well.

For example, perhaps your parent has really listened and apologized for saying negative things about your other parent to you when you were a child. As the two of you are feeling closer, you begin to launch into things you don't like about your stepparent, which then makes your parent get defensive. Before you realize it, you start arguing, and the important strides you just made get lost.

Stick with why you wanted the conversation and get what you are after. End the conversation, reserve other ideas that have come to mind for another day when you can be clear, and set up another successful meeting.

Don't let your parent use this opportunity to bring up an issue he or she wants to discuss with you. Whatever it is wasn't crucial enough for your parent to request a special meeting with you. If it's that important, say you can have a conversation about it at another time. You don't have to feel obligated to listen to a new issue your parent wishes to make just because he or she listened to you. You want this conversation to be a success, and keeping it short and on point is the way to get there.

Naturally, in the course of the conversation, there should be plenty of emotional dialogue and mutual listening. But it all needs to relate to *your* point and *your* goal. This means that your parent must be allowed to share feelings as well, but you do not have to listen to him or her go off on another issue.

If your parent is not responding as you'd hoped, try your best to return him or her to your original agenda of listening to you. Parents tend to get defensive, saying things like "You don't know the whole story" or "I don't remember that" or "I never knew that—why didn't you tell me?" Remind your parent that he or she doesn't need to get defensive, because you aren't on the attack. Repeat, as clearly as possible, what you are hoping to get out of the conversation.

After the Conversation

When you're done, if it's gone well, be appreciative and tell your parent that you hope you can continue to talk honestly on this level. If you walk away from the conversation not feeling as good as you had hoped, it is an indication that you wanted more from this conversation than you let yourself realize.

Maybe you received an apology and secretly, without even knowing it, you believed it was going to relieve your pain. Maybe you thought you'd be healed and are deeply let down because that's not what happened. It's okay and normal to feel this way. However, don't let it diminish the important conversation you just had. Maybe it didn't leave you feeling the way you wished, but it still went a long way in helping you to express yourself and be heard. Your voice is louder and clearer now, and that will help you to cultivate the inner voice you need to guide yourself in your life and growth.

If the conversation did not go well, consider why. If you lost your temper or moved off your agenda, understand that these life moments touch very deep places in all of us. Use this time to learn about yourself and reflect on how angry, hurt, or out of control you got. Remember that going back to the program at any time can help you to consider specific issues and grow from them.

If you believe the conversation's goals were not met because your parent was unwilling to listen to you, remind yourself that although it would've been nice, this conversation was never a necessary step in developing your ability to live your life the way you want. You are now taking control of your own life, and along the way you have to try different and new things. Some will prove helpful and others will not, but it's never a failure when you are in the process of change. This conversation might give you new insight about why you felt the way you did as a child. Be determined to learn about yourself from this conversation, no matter how it turns out.

If Your Parent Is Deceased

If your parent has passed away, this conversation can still take place in a different way. Write down the entire conversation as you'd like to have it take place. Make it as real as possible, following all the steps I've laid out in the chapter. On one day, write down your opening dialogue. On another day, write the response that you hope your parent would have said. If you can, place this conversation on your parent's grave or at another place related to his or her memory.

Even though your parent isn't there with you physically, I do believe that your parent's spirit lives on in some fashion. I truly believe that speaking to your parent in this way can elicit an accurate portrayal of how he or she would have responded in person.

Where to Go from Here

It can be liberating to get the feeling that your parent finally understands you. It will never take away the past, but it can be the start of a fresh adult relationship that is built on genuine feelings and honesty.

Try to create some concrete positive goals for the future. For example, consider setting up some time on a monthly basis when the two of you can be alone together. Plan on speaking regularly by phone. It doesn't always have to be for this type of serious conversation; it can just be to spend time together to work on and strengthen your bond. You can promote further bonding by offering to set up dates between your parent and your kids.

On the contrary, if at any time in the conversation you're unsure where you'd like the relationship to go, just stop there. The next step has to be whatever feels comfortable to *you*.

You may want to consider future discussions of specific issues that still trouble you. For example, 31 percent of the people in my survey said they are still bothered by their parents' inability to get along today, and 23 percent reported that they're still playing the role of mediator or messenger for their parents. These would be obvious issues to discuss openly with one or both of your parents—but only after you've reconnected and you feel sure they can hear you as an adult. Once that is accomplished, you can have further meetings and conversations to address these issues.

9

Getting Comfortable
with Love

Everlasting love doesn't come easily to adults who were children of divorce. Research shows that the greatest long-term effect of your parents' divorce on your life is your ability to find and sustain a loving relationship of your own. My own research bears this out. A resounding 72 percent of the adults in my survey said they have relationship issues. The majority said they lack self-confidence regarding love relationships, and 80 percent said they fear marriage and divorce.

I find this to be so sad. I've heard many, many painful stories in the last twenty-five years from adults who end up in situations similar to those of their divorced parents.

···

MELANIE'S STORY
"I Married a Man Like Dad"

The following story is quite typical of how we can reproduce the feelings of childhood in our adult romantic relationships without even realizing it. The next section is in Melanie's own words.

My mother and father never fought. They were completely distant. Every night they would sit quietly reading or watching television in separate rooms. I grew up feeling like there was literally no air in my house. I don't know why, but I was shocked when I was nine and my father went away on a trip and never came back. It was after two years of him "having to work out of state" that my mom told me they were getting divorced.

I realize now that when he "came home" during those two years, he was just visiting. Since they were so separate in the house when they were together, I didn't seem to miss anything when they were apart. Neither of them was particularly warm, but my mother definitely was the warmer of the two. Although she's no giant in the emotional realm, she was there and took care of us.

When I started dating seriously in college, I was always attracted to the life of the party. If the guy was the least bit shy or reserved, I didn't get near him. I knew why. I wasn't going to marry a man like my dad. No way. My man was going to be beyond colorful and would be breathing rainbows into my home. I was never going to get a divorce and hurt my children the way I was hurt, so I was sure I had the answer. I did for a while. I fell madly in love, and it was over the top. He was the star athlete in college. He was excited about everything, and I loved going along for the ride of a lifetime.

But after my first child was born, I wanted to be a mother and he wanted to continue being a fun-seeking teenager. When our second child was born, it dawned on me that I was feeling as stifled and lonely as when I was a child. I [had screwed things] up by finding someone just as selfish as my own father. All I wanted was to find the opposite, but he turned out to be just as selfish. We hadn't even hit the "seven-year itch" when I found out that the rainbows he introduced into my life turned out to be many different colors and shapes of women he'd been cheating with.

I went and asked my mother, and she confirmed that my dad had cheated on her for years as well, which explained some of her distant behavior. But I didn't know it, and I still married someone just the same. I've lived with two men since, because I'm terrified to ever marry or really commit to anyone again.

....

Your Opposite-Sex Parent

There are so many elements in how romantic relationships evolve, but here is one that you can bank on: your opposite-sex parent will largely dictate whom you will marry. It just makes sense. Your greatest familiarity with the opposite sex comes from your relationship—or lack thereof—with your own opposite-sex parent, regardless of your sexual orientation.

As you have now learned, every minute of your life as a child plays deeply into how you'll see and live your life as an adult. How loving, warm, and understanding or neglectful, punitive, and distant your opposite-sex parent was speaks volumes about how you felt deep down and what you learned to expect from life and lovers in the future.

It has nothing to do with whether you were happy or unhappy with what your parent did or didn't do. It's all about what feels familiar to you. As you now know, we don't like change. We will almost always choose a situation and a feeling that is commonly known to us rather than go out on a limb and try something that brings us a completely different emotion. This is why you might pull away from someone who is very loving to you if your opposite-sex parent was not very loving.

I know it seems counterintuitive, but it's the truth. It's not as easy as you think to accept love and caring from someone when you don't feel you deserve or are worthy of it because your parent didn't give you the loving feeling you deserved as a child.

The cognitive mind works in clever ways. When you leave childhood, you know what you don't like, so you tell yourself that you won't make the same mistakes. You are determined to marry someone who doesn't resemble your opposite-sex parent. Like Melanie, you marry someone who looks and seems very different. But changing the packaging isn't going to make it different.

You must focus on one thing: How does this person make me feel inside? That is the truest test of whether this relationship is healthier than the one you had with your opposite-sex parent. In Melanie's case, she focused only on what she saw externally. She wouldn't give a guy a second look if he wasn't the life of the party. That cuts out a lot of potentially great guys. She went for a personality that ended up being selfish. He was all about seeking behaviors that were self-serving. Melanie didn't realize that she was feeling just as out of control as she had felt as a child. This man seemed different because she was so drawn to the passionate lifestyle he led. But he never really tried to understand her any more than her father had. He never really tried to bring out her passion. He did what he wanted, and Melanie was happy to go along for the ride.

Another woman shared a story with me that on the surface seemed quite the opposite of Melanie's. Her dad was a violent screamer, and in order to resolve that, she married a very quiet guy. It wasn't long before she realized that she had gone for the safe option but had ended up with someone with no passion at all. He was numb, and she couldn't find any way to connect to him. Again, he *seemed* to be the opposite of her dad, but he made her feel very similarly disconnected. Her father did it through anger, and her husband did it through numbness, but they both made her feel lost and alone. She ended up in the situation she had sworn to herself a million times she'd never be in: divorced.

That Familiar Feeling

When entering a new relationship, always ask yourself, "How does this person make me feel?" You deserve to feel loved, worthy, and heard. If you don't feel all three, question the relationship. If you feel loved but realize you don't have much of a voice, or you have a voice but don't feel so loved, use this program to find deeper understanding. Too many women have said things to me like "I need a real man" or "He's too lovey and soft" or "There's not enough toughness in him." These tend to be code for "I'm looking for trouble."

Women tell me about guys who are too nice or cuddly. But their interpretation is based on their fathers, and they don't realize how much they're trying to drive themselves right back to where they started: feeling with their lovers the way they felt with their fathers. There is an incredible gravitational pull toward keeping that familiar father feeling alive and implanting it into the romantic relationship. I'm not talking about anything sexual or Freudian. I'm only opening your eyes to the emotional parts of your relationships.

Men are no different; they seek to go to the familiar mother relationship with their own love interests. Many men have told me that they broke up with a woman because she was too soft, kind, or loving, and they'll come up with clever reasons that these relationships didn't work. "She needs to be tougher" or "She needs to be more interesting" or "She needs to make more money" are all code for "I need someone more distant" who might be more reminiscent of how these men felt with their mothers. Again, nothing sexual is intended; I'm talking about the natural pull to create a familiar feeling that was developed in us from birth.

Making Comparisons

Of course, it is possible that your opposite-sex parent was wonderful to you, but divorce can wreak havoc on parenting skills and style. A failed marriage carries tremendous weight and sucks up so much emotional energy that it's not uncommon for a naturally good parent to become much less so as a result of many years of marital distress and divorce. So if your parent was good and made you feel loved, you will have a natural pull to find someone who makes you feel that way. But there is also a chance that your parent would have been a much better parent if he or she hadn't been absorbed in a troubled marriage. You have to take a really hard look at how you felt with this parent and then apply that to how you feel with your love interest.

Now is a good time to do a little journal writing and start think-ing about your love life. Write down and answer the following:

How did I feel about and respond to the love relationships of my past?

How do I feel about and respond to my current partner?

What are some similarities and differences between them?

How does my present relationship remind me of the feelings I had with my opposite-sex parent when I was a child?

Write down how you want to feel in your present relationship and list two ways in which you can go about feeling this way.

A Departure from the Norm

I have found anecdotally from those I have helped over the years that there were times in their lives when they might have departed from re-creating their relationships with their opposite-sex parents in their love interests. When people go to college or leave home in late adolescence, they often suddenly allow themselves to find new ways of living and feeling. It's as though they're rebelling against the reality of their earlier years and seeking a deeper level of meaning by going after different emotional experiences.

Many people have shared that they found someone during these years who made them feel wonderful, but the relationship didn't last. They typically don't really understand why it didn't last. Eventually, though, they almost always found someone who was much closer to making them feel the same way they did as a child. Familiarity has a powerful pull.

It might be helpful to look back on your earlier years. You too might discover that you have the ability to be different and feel different; if so, you can bring back some of those positive ways of living into your life today. If your relationships were better in your college days or your early adult life, consider why and what role you played in making them so. Use what you've learned to adopt those behaviors or emotional patterns in your life today.

Replicating Your Parents' Relationship

Your first and most influential model of marriage was, of course, the one your parents showed you. Just as you're likely to marry someone like your opposite-sex parent, you're just as likely to settle into a style of marriage that is familiar to you. That would be your parents' marriage.

I know that it's scary to imagine, and you've probably thought about it a million times before. You know you do not want your parents' marriage, but saying that and making it so are two completely different things. Day in and day out, every minute of your childhood, you soaked up messages about marriage like a sponge. You might have hated to hear your parents fight, but guess what? When you are faced with confrontation with your own spouse, your natural reaction will be to fight.

Why, you ask yourself, wouldn't your natural reaction be to calmly discuss your disagreements with your spouse? Why wouldn't you simply go over to your spouse, hold his or her hand, and lovingly talk about the burning issue? Knowing how to calmly discuss volatile topics is a skill, and it rarely comes naturally to someone who has grown up around confrontation. To possess this skill would be working against your natural tendencies.

You observed and lived in a home that presented a failed relationship. You most likely saw lots of bickering, fighting, and anger and very few loving gestures, warm physical touches and kisses, or kind conversations. You can probably remember being a child and thinking, "I never want to be this way" when you heard your parents fight or put each other down. But that just

isn't enough to teach yourself how to have a healthy, loving relationship. Left to your own devices, you'll repeat similar patterns.

It's necessary for you to seriously consider these messages
from childhood and learn how you are going to avoid them. You
might need to actually learn some specific skills to overcome
them. You may need to have these skills modeled for you through
conversations with friends or a counselor, by reading books, or by
attending seminars on the topic. It won't just happen because
you want it to. You need to *make* it happen.

Marrying a Healer

Susan Gregory Thomas, author of the memoir *In Spite of Everything*, shared with me one of her "aha!" moments one morning
while we were talking in the green room before we went on the
Today show to discuss her book. She said she had had extremely
unrealistic expectations going into her marriage. She had been
hurt and broken from her parents' divorce when she was a child,
so when she married, she wasn't just looking for a good man, she
was looking for a healer. She was looking for a god to alleviate
her pain. In her book she describes her unfortunate divorce,
which occurred even though she had promised herself she'd
never get a divorce.

Since you had a poor example of marriage in your childhood,
you are likely to have unrealistic expectations about marriage,
just as Susan did. You probably don't really know what you're
supposed to get out of marriage. I know you can say a bunch of
stuff—love, kindness, respect, et cetera, et cetera—but you don't
know how to translate that into real terms. You enter the great
unknown of marriage hoping to find something spectacular. You
might, like Susan, be expecting way too much. Marriage is not a
place to heal from a painful childhood. Your spouse is not meant
to reverse depression, anxiety, or feelings of worthlessness.

This expectation will sink any marriage, because the weight is just too heavy.

As an adult who was a child of divorce, you need to let your spouse know about your pain, and he or she should be willing to be there for you when you work to heal yourself through this program or by some other means. But you alone are in the driver's seat. Only *you* can make it happen.

Learn How to Fight Calmly

The worst part of divorce, through the eyes and ears of a child, is the fighting. This was the number one answer to the "worst part of my parents' divorce—before, during or after" in my research survey. Difficulty communicating is a problem in most marriages, so if you're conditioned to fighting from your parents' example, watch out. You will probably have to go a long way to turn this one around.

Fighting comes from the internal belief that "I have a right to feel angry and say whatever I want whenever I want." Before you have a chance to really consider what you want to say, however, the words have spilled out of your mouth and the verbal stabbing has begun. Fighting is a very unfortunate style of communication. People like to think of fighting as healthy and even justified at times; my personal favorite excuse is "Since every couple fights, I have the right to go to town on her [or him] whenever I like."

Fighting is an unhealthy response. You may have a right to feel hurt, sad, and, even angry at times. But you have a choice of how to handle and express it. What you choose to do about it is in your hands, and simply letting yourself scream, curse, name-call, or say purposely painful things is not justified.

This does not, of course, mean that it never happens in successful marriages. But in healthy marriages it happens infrequently, lasts for a very short time (because someone realizes it is unhealthy and unproductive), and does not cross the line into mean-spiritedness. The issues are then discussed calmly.

It's a given that your parents fought a lot, and this will give you added adrenaline to fight in your own marriage. Remember, though, that you're letting your autopilot take charge unless you learn to take a deep breath and cool down. Use this program to learn how to disagree, debate, and calmly discuss difficult matters with your spouse.

The Biggest Mistake of Failed Marriages

Make your marriage about your desire to love and be loved while always assessing how it feels. The biggest mistake in every failed relationship is waiting too long to deal with potentially troublesome issues. Failed marriages are created by partners who find excuses to not discuss or deal with issues while they are still small ones. There's a never-ending list of excuses: "We don't have much time now when the kids are small" or "We can't afford to do things that would make us happy" or "My spouse is under too much pressure from work."

When something isn't feeling right, do something immediately. I'm not suggesting you have to run to therapy at the drop of a hat, but at least talk about it together. If you aren't feeling connected, there's a problem. The problem might even be you, but that doesn't matter. The feeling of disconnection is a signal that you have to confront the problem and start discussing what you will try to do differently in order to make things better.

This is what every couple in a healthy marriage does. Every marriage is fraught with struggle. The healthy couple finds ways, and isn't afraid to invent ways, to feel connected going through life and struggles together. This can be you, but only if you make it so.

10

Embrace Trust and Honesty

Children of divorce have serious issues with trust and honesty, and these issues follow them into adulthood. My research found that 69 percent of adults who were children of divorce believe that their parents' divorce has affected their ability to trust others, especially in love relationships. And 43 percent said the number one memory that still lingers with them is that one or both of their parents lied to them about issues involving the divorce.

A child's loss of trust is a common side effect of divorce. Much of what you know about life you learned from your parents. They were there to teach you how to walk, speak, eat, pick out your clothes, and brush your teeth. They chose your schools and guided your education. Children depend on their parents to help them, teach them, and furnish them with the tools and information to navigate life. So when children start to think that their parents are lying to them, it is very discomforting.

Once you find out that a parent purposely lies to serve his or her own needs, you begin to worry about your very basic understanding of life. You may not consciously be aware of it, but this type of betrayal affects you deeply on an emotional level. It may still bother you and be the reason you question how you deal with trust today.

Fact versus Opinion

Trust and honesty are tender issues for adults who were children of divorce. It is important that those who love you understand your need for honesty. Because of this, I believe that you need to adopt a zero-tolerance policy on lying in your love relationships.

The first rule is to always be honest and open about your behavior. Neither of you should ever lie about where you have been, what has been happening, or what you have been doing. For example, if you purchased something, don't lie about how much money you spent. If you forgot to drop off the dry cleaning or the bank deposit, don't try to cover it up.

To lie about real life is to distort reality. It is dangerous to any relationship, but especially for adults who were children of divorce.

This also means there can be no lying about things that happened in the past, before the two of you met or became a couple. Get delicate issues out in the open. If you ask or are asked about something in your past that you don't want to reveal or don't like to talk about, have an understanding about how to handle that. Respect each other's feelings in the matter. If you or your mate says you don't feel comfortable discussing something, then the other one shouldn't press the issue. You are only risking an argument or forcing a lie.

You also need to be completely clear where the line is drawn between honesty and dishonesty. There is a difference between fact and opinion. Information about an action or an inaction involves facts, not opinions.

If one of you is asked a question that could lead to hurt feelings—how the other looks in an outfit, spoke during a meeting, or enjoyed dinner—I believe it's fair game to give a diplomatic answer or even lie about your opinion. It's okay because these questions do not involve facts; another person could have a completely different opinion from yours in answering these questions. Also, recognize that opinions are fleeting. Minds can change when more thought is put into the question. This is not distorting reality. If hurting each other's feelings is an issue between the two of you, then being less than truthful about your opinion is acceptable.

By no means am I suggesting that you can really go to town lying to each other just to make each other feel good. You need to be able to depend on each other's honesty to help you make decisions. Relationships are built on trust. Honesty and trust go hand in hand. The two of you should clearly know where you stand and agree to do your best.

What's on Your Mind, Honey?

Honesty becomes a slippery slope when it involves your private thoughts, daydreams, and fantasies. These kinds of mental activities are ever changing, depending on your mood of the moment. Sometimes we are not even aware of what exactly we're thinking. Remember, though, that your mind is always active, even when you're totally quiet. So it won't be uncommon for your mate to suddenly spring the question "What's on your mind, honey?"

Discuss with your mate how you want to deal with this type of honesty. For example, "Do you ever think of having sex with another person?" is a very loaded question. Perhaps you and your mate can agree to bow out of conversations that are going to incite issues. Or you could agree not to ask such questions. If it happens, allow some leeway in what is considered an honest answer.

I believe the healthiest approach is for each of you to have the option of saying something like this:

> I'm not going there, and not because it's an answer you don't want to hear, but because it's not fair to start floating around my thoughts as though they are real in any way. I can have lots of fleeting thoughts that mean nothing to my reality. If you want to know whether I've planned to have, or have had, sex with anyone else, the answer to that is an emphatic *no*. If your question is your way of saying you're worried about my fidelity, then let's discuss that directly.

The most important point is for you and your mate to discuss all of these issues so there is clarity and understanding on all matters of honesty.

Let History Be Your Barometer

Trust issues from childhood can cause two completely opposite problems: not trusting your mate enough when you should, and trusting someone too much when he or she hasn't properly gained your trust. Consider the facts of your relationship and do your best to act on that history. Don't listen to what someone says; consider what his or her past actions have shown. If history says your lover lies, then expect to continue getting lies until he or she proves otherwise. Trust the untrustworthy to continue being untrustworthy!

However, if your mate is trustworthy but you keep challenging his or her trust, then it's up to *you* to change *your* attitude. Use what you've learned through the Re-Right Your Past program to help you work through it. You don't want your insecurities from childhood to come between you and a loving partner and cause you to miss out on love.

11

Infidelity

Reconciling the Ultimate Betrayal

As a child of divorce, you are likely to have issues about infidelity. You may fear that your spouse is going to cheat on you, and you may worry that you could end up being a cheater yourself. It's no wonder. Infidelity is at the heart of a lot of divorces. According to my research, 70 percent of adults who were children of divorce say they know or have reason to suspect that one or both of their parents were unfaithful in their marriage. And 43 percent said they found out about the cheating from the parent who was cheated on. What a sad mess! And this has been your life!

Adults who were children of divorce are primed for anxiety and issues related to cheating in their romantic relationships. Infidelity is not something foreign that happens to others. You probably believed or were told that it was the cause of your family's demise. You probably know better than most how much cheating can destroy a marriage and what a powerful enemy it can be. Unfortunately, this doesn't commonly translate into your creating wonderful relationships. Instead, it has left you with a lot of anxiety about falling in love. You might even be avoiding true love for fear of heartbreak.

You might also be worried about yourself. You might think that you can't be true to just one person. As the saying goes, the apple doesn't fall far from the tree. Familiarity with this issue is part of your mental map.

If cheating was going on in your natal family when you were growing up, there's a chance it could occur in the family you create as an adult. To avoid it from ruining your marriage or relationship, you need to seriously consider what cheating has meant to your life and what you're going to do to make sure it doesn't crawl into your bed.

Four Key Issues to Keep in Mind

As a child of divorce, you experienced certain things that will almost certainly cause some complicated feelings and issues in your life. Even after you complete the program, you should keep these specific issues in the forefront of your mind, where you can manage them. You will need to focus on particular issues to be sure you're not allowing them to negatively affect your life. The primary issues—infidelity, parenting, money, and sadness—are addressed in the remaining chapters.

I don't have a single simple answer for you that will make these issues go away, but I offer many suggestions that I hope will help you along your way. The best I can promise is that the more you are aware of these issues and think and talk about them, the less they will negatively affect your life.

The Best Rules for Avoiding Infidelity

Infidelity is so wrong that it's a topic most people avoid. Instead, everyone pretends that everyone in a relationship agrees to the same rule: no sex outside the relationship. Furthermore, something you may not realize, but what I have found through my research, is that the majority of cheating involves an emotional attachment. It's not "just sex"; it's more than just a one-night stand. Frequently, long- and short-term friendships build and lead to sexual relationships. And almost always, the spouse will sense trouble brewing before he or she feels the knife in the back.

Do you know how to pick up on the signs of infidelity? Do you know how to deal with these signs? If you sense your lover becoming distant, do you know how to handle the situation without pushing him or her further away? If you're feeling susceptible to cheating, do you know what to do about it? (And I'm not talking about giving in to it!)

There is one thing for sure: doing nothing in any of these situations is the best way to repeat history and refresh deep wounds.

If you believe that cheating was going on in your parents' marriage when you were a child, infidelity is a topic you need to talk about openly with your mate. As you enter a serious relationship, discuss and develop guidelines for how both of you will manage your relationships with members of the opposite sex. It is not enough to say things like "If you cheat, it's over." There are many ways of being intimate with the opposite sex that don't involve physical cheating. Here are some things to consider:

- *Private time.* Is it okay for either of you to go out for a meal alone with someone of the opposite sex? How do you feel about close male-female friendships? What about conversations in online chat rooms? For each of these, it may make a huge difference if it happens once in a while or once a week. But the two of you need to discuss and decide this.

- *Physical contact.* Is it okay if either of you dances with someone else? How do you feel about greeting someone with a hug or a kiss on the cheek? Is it okay to be around someone who you both know would like to pursue one of you, and if you agree that it's all right to be around this person, what will you do to avoid anything inappropriate?

- *Work-related relationships.* Do you work late hours with a certain colleague? Do you take long car rides or otherwise travel with this colleague? Do you stay in the same hotel? How much of your relationship crosses the line from work into friendship?

- *Former lovers.* Is it okay to stay in touch or get in touch with former lovers? Is it okay to get together for lunch or dinner with a former lover who is passing through town?

I am not saying what the answers should be. I'm only suggesting that you use these questions as guidelines to have healthy discussions in your love relationship. The most important rule is this: if something occurs, it is open for discussion. For example, if your old boyfriend calls you out of the blue, telling your mate about it the very same day allows you to discuss it instead of fighting about it later.

What to do about any of these issues will be different for each couple, but it is important that you come to some agreement. If there are gray areas, then at least agree on them and disclose them if or when they come up. Different scenarios might require different responses. Knowing that neither of you will be blindsided by hiding something will give your relationship greater security.

Cheating Signs

One of the greatest insights I culled through my infidelity research is that cheaters give signs that they are *about* to cheat. Unfortunately, most spouses either don't notice them or offer excuses that cause the signs to be swept under the rug. Here are the top five signs:

1. Spending less time talking and just being together.
2. Spending more time away from home, whether for work, a hobby, or some other excuse.
3. Having diminished sexual activity.
4. Being out of touch, such as not answering the cell phone or spending too much time "at the store."
5. Starting more fights.

It doesn't matter which side of the fence you're on. If you notice these signs, don't hide your head in the sand. It doesn't mean that cheating has already occurred, but they are risk factors, just as surely as high blood pressure and high cholesterol are risk factors for heart disease. It says the two of you are moving away from each other as lovers. Now is the time to deal with it.

Let's Talk

Obviously, broaching the subject is just the beginning. But making an effort to address these signs is the only way to deter cheating, and talking will lead you to create a better relationship. Unfortunately, most people hide their heads in the sand and hope for it all to go away. It's the wrong approach.

Most people who notice these signs worry and fret rather than talk about the problem. They hold it all in and don't bring it up until the tension has built to a breaking point: "I've been trying to get you on your cell phone all day! Where have you been?" Or "You rejected me sexually again last night. Is there someone else?" It becomes accusatory and leads to a fight. But if you bring it up at a calm moment with the intention of finding concrete answers to how the two of you will put more focus on love in your relationship, you will not fight about it anymore.

If you see any of these signs in your relationship, bring the issue up and talk about practical ideas for reconnecting: finding time and space for more friendship, sex, and experiences together. Don't let life—work, kids, bills—dictate how much love you have in your marriage. Remember how destructive cheating was for your family and vow to put into action real changes that will make your marriage stronger.

If you need more help with this issue, I've written three books about relationships, and each one offers a great deal of discussion as well as concrete plans for avoiding cheating while developing an honest, trusting marriage. These books are *Emotional Infidelity: How to Affair-Proof Your Marriage and 10 Other Secrets to a Great Relationship*, *The Truth about Cheating: Why Men Stray and What You Can Do to Prevent It*, and *Connect to Love: The Keys to Transforming Your Relationship*.

12

The Insecure Parent

Family judges are fond of the saying "In criminal court, we see bad people at their best. In family court, we see good people at their worst."

Caring for children is difficult under the best of circumstances. So imagine what it was like for your own parents, who had to maneuver through a failing relationship culminating in divorce and its ensuing emotional and financial issues. Under such circumstances, having enough energy left to tend to rambunctious kids is a tall order.

Even if you had two wonderful, loving, and caring parents, the strain of marital strife interferes with the ability to parent well. It's no surprise that my research found that adults who were children of divorce have concerns about their own parenting skills. It's a natural backlash from going through a childhood marred and disrupted by divorce.

Sometimes children of divorce are afraid to have children of their own because they are so unsure of their own ability to parent well. If their parents weren't very good at the job, how are they going to know what's best? After all, parents are role models. In addition, children of divorce don't want to ever put their kids through what they went through, so they are nagged by the thought of "What if something goes wrong in my marriage?"

It's an unfortunate fact: if you were a child of divorce, the odds are that you're going to have a harder time honing your own parenting skills. Don't be surprised if you find yourself working a lot harder to be a caring parent than the parent next door has to.

My research shows that there are a few residual issues from your childhood that can negatively affect your own style of parenting. They are the focus of this chapter.

How You Were Told about Your Parents' Divorce

Because I am the author of *Helping Your Kids Cope with Divorce the Sandcastles Way*, parents about to divorce frequently consult me about the best way to share the unfortunate news with their children. The book has a chapter on a detailed method of sharing this news in a way that will be least hurtful.

The number one rule is that both parents should be together to tell the children. At the moment of the family's breakup, it's important for children to see a sense of solidarity and unity to help them feel confident that their parents are working this through as two cooperative adults. It is a moment that is hard to forget, for both the parents and the children.

To have the news broken any other way just makes it that much more scary to kids. Unfortunately, it happens the right way much too seldom. My survey found that only 19 percent of parents broke the news together to their kids. Even sadder is that 20 percent said their parents never told them about the divorce at all; they found out about it by overhearing their parents blurt it out while fighting or through some unforgettable event such as divorce papers being served at home. Another 23 percent said the news was broken to them by one parent. The rest weren't sure or were too young to remember how they found out.

A lack of clarity from parents at this tragic moment can translate into confusion for adults who were children of divorce. They may see a gray area when it's time to be clear and open with their own children. As a child of divorce, you might try to hide certain things from your children to protect them. You have to ask yourself, "Would they be better served knowing?"

For example, if the two of you had an argument last night and are a bit cool to each other today, do you say something to your children, who might sense something is up? If your children are old enough to understand, the answer is yes, it's a good idea. Perhaps you could tell them that the two of you had a bit of an argument last night but that you'll work things out soon enough. This gives your children a sense that the tension they're feeling in the house is real but that it has nothing to do with them and that the adults in the house recognize it and are planning on dealing with it. If things were often hidden from you as a child, this is a skill that might not come easy for you.

Now imagine the same scenario, but this time you share too much information about last night's fight. While getting ready for school, one of you tells your children that the two of you fought until 4 a.m. over Grandma's decision to move down the block—a problem, you emphasize, that isn't going to go away soon. You do this in the spirit of being up front and honest with your kids, because your parents were certainly not up front and honest with you. This approach, however, is no healthier than hiding the argument. Both approaches result in too much stress for the children.

There is no one methodology of parenting. We all learn as we go, but you need to stay very clear about your weak spots so you can get better at managing them. You need to keep your own childhood issues in mind in order to be certain that these issues are not negatively affecting your ability to be a good parent. If you are presently in the process of divorce, make sure you take every step to learn how to go through it with as little trauma as possible for your children.

Honesty Is Often a Delicate Issue

So much of parenting is about diplomacy: knowing how and when to teach your children about life. When you've been lied to as a child in ways that were hurtful, it can play huge games with your sense of clarity. One area of struggle is knowing how to deal honestly with your own children.

You may choose to never pretend there's a Tooth Fairy or a Santa Claus. You may choose to be brutally honest about your feelings and opinions on everything, even if it hurts your kids. After all, honesty is the best policy; you know what dishonesty did to you when you were a kid. Or you may end up being as closed and as comfortable about lying as your parents were.

What's going to be your policy on honesty with your children? It is worth the time and energy to talk it through with your spouse. This is very likely to be a concern of yours. As I noted in chapter 10, 43 percent of adults who were children of divorce say they are still bothered today by their belief that one or both of their parents lied to them. This presents quite a challenge for your own parenting techniques, because honesty in itself is complicated. After all, you can't always be honest with your children. If your five-year-old asks you how babies are made or what does *sex* mean, you don't want to get too graphic, so you deftly answer the question in a general way and withhold a great deal of information. Is this lying? You may create a story about a stork. Is this a harmful lie?

Honesty is crucial for children, but you should also feel comfortable withholding things that you believe would be harmful to your children, as long as they won't be finding them out from someone else. Here are a few principles to keep in mind when dealing with this delicate issue:

- *Avoid lying.* If your children ask you a question about a matter you don't wish to discuss, instead of outright lying, tell them it is a subject you do not want to discuss. They might not like it, but it is much better than a lie. You might want to explain that there are certain things that are too personal to discuss, that the answer includes information about someone else whose confidence you don't want to betray, or that the subject is inappropriate at your children's ages. As long as you don't use this rationale constantly, your children will probably be able to accept it. It will leave them trusting that you are open and up front.

- *Don't promise your children anything you can't follow through on.* It is much better to say something like "I'm planning on taking you to Disney World" instead of "I promise to take you to Disney World." Even when you think a promise is best for your children's well-being, don't make one unless you are certain you will follow through. Empty promises like "We'll never get a divorce" or "I'm going to live to be one hundred" may sound harmless at the time, but they make an impression on children. If the circumstances turn out differently, it can pain the children even more.

- *Consider being more diplomatic.* If you and your spouse have been fighting and you children ask if you're going to get a divorce, say, "We have no plans to divorce, and we're working on our issues so that we stay focused on making a good marriage." Pretending that the fight is not a fight is not a good strategy. When these types of meaningful questions are asked, your initial response should be to find out what is behind the question and where the concern is coming from. Ultimately, there are questions you can't answer. When this is the case, make it clear to your children.

- *Be the first to tell your children you lied.* No child feels good about learning that Santa isn't real from another kid who makes your child feel stupid for believing it in the first place. If you choose to carry on the Santa, Easter Bunny, and Tooth Fairy traditions, be sure to tell your children the truth before they hear it from other kids. This way they'll understand that it was all a fun game aimed at giving them joy. Tell them it is the tradition of millions of families so your kids understand that it is a charade in the name of family fun that is accepted by society.

If you have lied to your children in the past, get it out in the open before someone else does. For example, if you told your daughter when she was ten that you did not call her teacher when she was having issues at school when you actually did call the teacher, let your daughter know you did at a later date, before the teacher mentions it at her middle school graduation.

You have the right to lie when you think it's best for your children, but letting them live long-term with a lie can have terrible repercussions. You can explain later why you lied and why you felt it was in their best interests. It may be a very difficult conversation to have, and it may lead to some upsetting moments, but it is a healthier approach than maintaining the lie and hoping your children never find out.

An Ongoing Self-Check

Honesty must be an ongoing personal discussion for every child of divorce who is now a parent. The sadness brought on by mistrusting your parents is not something that easily goes away. It can affect your own ability to parent. If you take the time to seriously consider the importance of open communication, you'll be sure to find your unique way of making sure your personal relationship with your children is based on honesty and integrity.

13

Money Issues

A Common Bond

Many of you were too young to really understand how your parents' divorce affected your lives financially. I will bet, however, that the divorce didn't leave you better off.

According to my research, only about 7 percent of children of divorce experienced an increase in their standard of living after their parents' divorce. About 25 percent of families maintained the status quo. For the rest, the standard of living took a nosedive.

Money is a major issue in the aftermath of divorce, even in families that are well-to-do. More often than not, when one parent moves out and the divorce papers are signed, a for-sale sign goes up on the house's lawn—out of need, not desire. Since the breadwinner has traditionally been the father, this usually meant that the mother had to find a job and that she and the kids had to make do with less, even with child support payments coming in.

The landscape has changed somewhat; the mother most likely already has a job, quite possibly a well-paying one. Still, a basic fact remains: two households cannot live as cheaply as one, even if one of them is a one-person household. Someone always gets shortchanged, and it is usually the parent with multiple mouths to feed. This usually means that the mother, who almost always gets custody, is left with a shrinking piggybank. It leaves a lasting impression on the kids and gives them a skewed relationship to money.

Money is the root of survival. It's impossible to live without it. The lack of it creates anxiety and leads to desperation. It is the motivation for most crimes and the number one cause of friction in marriages, but it is also the chief source of friction in divorce. Making and managing money are at the heart of so many issues in life that I can't even begin to list them here. However, it is important for you, as an adult who was a child of divorce, to pay attention to your relationship with money. One thing is certain: like almost everything else, how you feel about money today has a lot to do with your childhood.

Money means much more than having an extra toy or two. It determines the quality of life: the type of home and neighborhood you live in, the education your children receive, who your friends are, and your general sense of control. Money equals power, and as much as we all want it, we don't necessarily do the things it takes to have it.

It's likely that when you go through the Re-Right Your Past program, your current financial status will surface as an issue, possibly even a major one, so I'd like you to get your journal and do a little reflecting about money. This isn't an instant quiz; I want you to ponder several questions over the next few days, then come back and write your responses. Think about these issues and write your response to each one in your journal:

- What was the message my parents gave me about money?
- Did one parent use money as a weapon or a threat to me or to my other parent?
- Did one parent have more power because he or she controlled the money?
- What is my general approach toward finances?
- What do I enjoy most about money: making it, spending it, or saving it? How does this relate to my parents' relationship to money?

The chances are that your answers have created some anxiety, because you can now see that money was a driver of the friction in your family life growing up. It is quite common for divorced parents to use money as a weapon or a threat against the former spouse as a way to "get in good" with the kids. It's insidious, because a child doesn't see the manipulation at play. The child experiences it as a moment of "truth" and a source of comfort—"Look what Daddy bought me!"—and his or her heart is saying, "Daddy still loves me." It's the beginning of a skewed image that money can buy love, even though we all eventually realize that this is impossible.

....

KALIN'S MONEY ISSUE
I Was Doing It for My Kids

Kalin's story is a classic example. Money issues almost ruined her marriage. When she was eleven, Kalin's dad moved out, and within one month he had announced that he was going to marry his new girlfriend. Suddenly Kalin found herself in a very familiar child-of-divorce position: she resided primarily with her mom, while her stepsiblings and eventual half siblings lived full-time with her dad.

Kalin loved and deeply missed her dad. She loved her mom and enjoyed living with her, but she couldn't understand why other children got to live with her dad and she couldn't. To make matters worse, Kalin soon became aware of huge financial discrepancies between her life and that of her stepsiblings. After the divorce, Kalin could no longer return to the private school and the camp that she had enjoyed. But, remarkably, her stepsiblings were enrolled at the same school and camp, even though they had never gone there previously. For a while, Kalin believed they were called her *step*siblings because they had literally stepped into her life and taken it over.

When as a teenager she confronted her dad about it, he simply responded that he'd given her mom more than enough money and that if she wanted to "hoard" it all, that wasn't his problem.

Needless to say, Kalin grew up determined to make sure that her children would never suffer this way financially. At times she fought bitterly with her husband, demanding that her children have the best of everything and never be made to feel less than or have to go without. As a result, the bills piled up, creating both family and financial stress. Kalin was appalled when she found herself hurtling toward divorce with three children and the serious possibility of a financial meltdown. Her husband's primary issue was her "overzealous" determination to spend money on the children in ways that made him feel uncomfortable. He was adamant that they couldn't afford the lifestyle, and he also believed it was unhealthy for their children to be raised in such a manner.

Kalin refused to realize what she was doing until her fourteen-year-old daughter told her that she'd rather go to public school than see her parents divorce. Kalin then realized that although she was doing everything for the sake of her children, she wasn't preserving the most meaningful part of her children's lives: their family unity. Her childhood had caused such scars that she became focused solely on healing them while not seeing the forest for the trees.

A Lesson for Us All

There's a lesson in this story for every child of divorce. Be willing to confront your own childhood divorce issues related to money. Examine how they are creating your personal style of money management for yourself and your family. Put this under the microscope and examine whether it is something you need to change.

We all want a better life for our children than we had ourselves, and this is especially true for adults who were children of divorce. But ask yourself, "Am I keeping this in perspective?" People who try to live beyond their means are generally very insecure people. People who come from broken families generally grow up building a trail of insecurities. It is no coincidence that adults who were children of divorce are well represented among the many people who have a problem managing money. Taking fiscal responsibility is an important link in finding your truth and creating change.

14

Your Best Self-Help Tools

As part of my research, I wanted to know what people had already done that brought them some relief and healing from their parents' divorce. The number one answer, by a long shot, was "nothing." That wasn't surprising, since I was planning on writing this book because I knew there was a lot of pain and few answers. There were, however, several mechanisms that people found helpful.

Start Talking

An astounding 53 percent of the people in my study said that they did not talk about their parents' divorce with anyone when they were children, and 78 percent said they did not talk about it as adults. Another 22 percent said that they never talked about it, as children *or* as adults. Of those who did talk about it, 68 percent found that doing so was very helpful.

It's remarkable how alone a child of divorce feels. When you grow up, you hear statistics about how many millions of children have divorced parents. You'd think that as a child you would have felt more normal coming from a divorced home. If you add to this the number of homes where there aren't good marriages but the parents stay together anyway, you're definitely in the majority. But when you're a kid, you're not looking at the world of other children. You can only see your own, and all you know is that your world is being torn apart, so you think there must be some-thing terribly wrong with your family.

Every child of divorce feels uniquely isolated and abnormal. This is why I developed the Sandcastles program for children of divorce. I wanted children to see other kids their ages who were just like them. These kids enter the room feeling abnormal, but they instantly realize they are as normal as everyone else in the group. There is safety in numbers. But most children only experience a sense of loss without feeling that there are many others out there just like them.

This is why the majority of children do not talk to anyone about divorce; it is simply too embarrassing and strange. They think that if they talk about it, they'll create a deeper chasm between them and the rest of their world. It's bad enough that they already feel so different; talking about it will just make oth-ers find them even odder, they think.

Talking is the most useful tool we have for healing. It is so powerful. Our ability to speak is what separates us from the ani-mal world. Through speech we connect to others. We can instantly feel uplifted from one conversation because feeling understood by someone is crucial to our existence and to the way we heal. We live around others because of this absolute need to feel that another person "gets" us and we are not alone.

Even as adults, many children of divorce are hesitant to talk because they worry others will consider them complainers. They fear that people will say, "Get over it." The idea that divorce must not be harmful because millions of people do it is a tragic societal error. To believe otherwise would be to admit that a humongous part of the population comes to adulthood with built-in issues. But it's the truth, and finding someone you can trust to understand can be extremely helpful. It won't solve your problems, but it'll give you a sense of having a voice and of being understood, something children of divorce often lose in childhood.

You're not a complainer. You've really been affected by your parents' divorce, and sharing that with someone you love and trust will help you. They don't have answers, but they have a loving understanding that will be like magic to your existence. You can find your own answers by reading and using this book. However, you will always need to feel connected to someone, and sharing your childhood feelings is an important part of who you are. So start talking. As I suggested in chapter 8 about your parents, let people know what you want and don't want from them. Explain that you want understanding, not advice, and you'll get their genuine empathy, something you have always deserved.

Deal with Your Sadness and Depression

Children of divorce have a propensity to be depressed. In my research, 80 percent said their parents' divorce seriously contributed to episodes of severe sadness or depression in adulthood.

These episodes are often overwhelming and don't have to make sense. You know you "shouldn't" be so sad, but that knowledge doesn't help you or anyone else to just snap out of it. I hope that this process has helped, or will help, you to make your life happier and get to the root of the issues, which is your best defense against depression. But if you find yourself in the dumps today, consider these potential remedies:

- *Get some exercise.* Various forms of exercise have scientifically been proven to eliminate depression and improve mood. Anyone who exercises regularly can experience a high during a workout that makes you feel good all day. When you are down, pull yourself out of bed and get moving. Even a thirty-minute walk makes a difference. It's worth pushing yourself on this one, because it will most likely take the edge off a bad or depressed mood and allow you to see life more clearly.

- *Commune with nature.* Studies show that just looking at a picture of nature can lift your spirits. Being outdoors in nature, even if you're just sitting or walking, can give you a mental lift. Weather permitting, create consistent daily time to gaze at a nature scene. You are part of nature, and feeling part of something bigger can give you a feeling of being grounded and belonging.

- *Reach out to others.* What are friends for? They're not there just for the fun they bring into your life; they are there to help you through the rough patches, too. Your friends and your family love you and want to help you. You just need to let them know that you need their help. When you are down, it is time to ask for their help. You may want them to listen to your issues, or you may want them to distract you from your issues and just take you out to do something fun. Leaning on the love of others is something all of us should do. This is your time of need.

- *Plan something fun.* All of us need something to look forward to. So if fun in your life isn't happening naturally, make it so. Create plans to do something that will give you pleasure. Knowing something wonderful is awaiting you can ease your difficult moments.

- *Learn a breathing technique.* Were you ever told to take a deep breath before someone delivered bad news? Breathing techniques are calming, and there are a variety of them that are proven anxiety breakers. The time to learn about and practice breathing techniques is not when you need them but rather before you need them.

One that I use and tell others to use is color breathing. Close your eyes and picture the most pleasing color to you in the form of a small, cool (or warm, if you prefer) steam cloud in front of your face. For the next minute or so, concentrate as you slowly breathe this comforting air into your lungs and let it spread through your head, your shoulders and arms, your torso, and your legs and feet, until you feel it filling your entire self. Afterward, visualize a scene of your life that is particularly loving and beautiful, or any scene that puts a smile on your face.

Practice this, or any other breathing technique you might learn about, as you go to sleep every night, so that you get used to it and are comfortable doing it. This way, when you do have a sense of darkness enveloping you, you'll be practiced and ready to dispel it with a breathing exercise.

Consider Therapy

Depression is nothing to ignore. There's no doubt that therapy is a helpful tool for getting over the trauma of your parents' divorce. Yet my survey found that only 18 percent had seen a therapist as a child, and 40 percent had seen one as an adult. If the advice I offer in this book hasn't helped to give you a lift or get a handle on what's troubling you in life (or you've been too down to even try any of the techniques), then you should seek professional help.

If you want to consider medication as an additional help, you'll need to see a psychiatrist, who is a medical doctor with a specialty is understanding the mind and psychotherapeutic medicines. I don't believe that medication without therapy is a wise choice, in most cases. Every medication has potential side effects. You'll need to weigh them against the side effects of your depression: How is it affecting your marriage, your parenting, or your job?

There are different forms of therapy, far too many to discuss here. To determine which kind is best for you, ask yourself what you'd like to get out of therapy. Are you looking for the relief that can come just from someone genuinely listening, validating your feelings, and helping you to feel normal and accept your feelings? This can be accomplished through counseling.

It might seem odd that you're paying a stranger to listen to you and validate you, but let's face it, in today's fast-paced world, it's not easy to sit for an hour and chat uninterrupted. Since the therapy is all about you, the therapist can focus on your feelings without any interruption. The therapist is not concerned about his or her own feelings about your issues and can remain completely focused on you and your feelings. This will make you feel truly heard and understood.

Finding a stranger to talk to can be better than talking to someone you know, because there is no hidden agenda with a therapist. Suppose you tell your spouse that you are anxious about being at family holiday parties because they bring back memories of childhood trauma around that season. Your spouse will be thinking about many things besides how unfortunate it is for you. He or she will be thinking about how this will affect this year's family holiday party and how you can be coaxed into attending a full weekend of activities. This muddies the "please just understand me" waters, and you may not feel that you're being fully understood. Granted, your spouse should be working to get to a place where he or she can fully focus on you, but a therapist doesn't have to work at all to do that, because he or she is fully there for you right from the start.

If you want more from therapy than just an empathetic listener, that brings up the question of how a therapist will help you. Unfortunately, therapy is far from an exact science, so each therapist has his or her own method of helping. You know mine from this book (and maybe my other books); I look for deep connections and changes. Many therapists don't do this, however, so it's up to you to openly discuss your goals right from the start; find out the therapist's methodology and how long he or she thinks it will take for you to reach your goals. You're not looking for an exact answer as much as an indication of how the therapist thinks that he or she can help you.

After every few sessions, ask your therapist how your therapy is going and discuss your goal for the next few sessions. Therapy can be incredibly helpful, but the therapist doesn't do the work for you. You need to be in charge of your own healing. You're in the driver's seat.

Be Diligent about Your Mental Health

All of us feel sadness from time to time. Since you are a child of divorce, recognizing how childhood has led you to feel sad and/or have episodes of depression is crucial for finding your way back to happiness. Don't wait until you're in a funk to create a plan. Enlist the help of your loved ones or a professional. Your spouse will often notice the beginning signs of emotional trouble in you before you do. You can work together to use that moment to stave off depression before it starts.

Religion Works for Many

Many of you have found religion to be of enormous help in managing your issues from childhood. Religion offers so many positives, and some are uniquely suited for adults who were children of divorce. Feeling a spiritual and inspirational connection to God can go a long way in dealing with a childhood affected by divorce.

Many of you spent your childhood experiencing one or both parents not being focused on you and not understanding you. Religion can give you the feeling that your ultimate parent, God, is listening and connecting with you. It can serve as an adult antidote to feeling unworthy of being heard. Prayer is another form of talking. There's nothing like uninterrupted time with God, whose cell phone is always on vibrate.

Religion can also offer a collective community focused on similar altruistic actions. For you as a child, one of the most painful parts of your parents' divorce was feeling the loss of your most important community: your family. Religious communities can feel like family and are often unconditionally accepting of others. This can go a long way in reminding you that you are valuable and acceptable, that you deserve to be a part of something special.

There are many different types of institutions that represent many different religions. Consider visiting one and getting involved. Sometimes you have to try different places before you find the one that offers the feeling you are trying to get from the experience. Don't judge all religious institutions by one, and especially not by the one you attended in childhood. As an adult you have to be in charge of finding the relationships that make you healthy.

Religion can be a wonderful means by which to feel loved, accepted, and heard. It can also give you a sense of purpose and value because of what you can do for others.

Epilogue

This book has most likely been an intense journey for you. You have probably felt some sadness as you reminded yourself of many painful issues, and you have had insights and made discoveries about yourself that have led you to greater emotional freedom. As with any process, there are always peaks and valleys, but you'll stick with it because you are recognizing change already and know that it is leading to a healthier you.

Sometimes, in the sad moments brought up by this book, you might have felt forlorn, because even though you knew that times weren't always good for you growing up, you believed at the time that they were better than they actually were. You might have believed that your parents understood you more than you now believe they did, or that the memories you swept under the rug really weren't so bad. Now you may feel sad knowing the harsh reality of your childhood, even though you are better for it and have been able to finally take control of your life.

There is a sort of grieving period when we go through a process like Re-Right Your Past that makes us grow and realize things are not what we made them seem. But to overcome this sad reality, remember this: *You are grieving the fantasy, not the reality.* You are not now dealing with the loss of your parental love or understanding; you are dealing only with the loss of the fantasy that you built around believing that things were different than they really were. You haven't lost anything in real time, only the express childlike desire to want to minimize the pain and believe in your parents in a way that was unhealthy for you.

The Worst Part of Divorce

The resounding message that came out of my research is that a childhood enmeshed in divorce can make you feel unworthy. Perhaps the worst feeling in life is shame; children of divorce commonly report it.

My intention in writing this book was to give you back your life, to convince you that you are worthy, and as much as I wish I could just tell you and have you believe me, I needed to help you get there on your own. If only it were an easy journey; but it's not. Reversing such a deep sense of loss can happen only with great work and insight on your part. Believe me when I tell you that it can be done. I have heard from thousands of people who have changed their lives and created the ones they choose to live. I believe in you, and now it's time for you to believe in yourself.

Whenever you question what you should do or how you should feel, just consider what you would tell your friend or your child if he or she were in the same situation. Whatever that answer is, you deserve no less. Always use this technique to keep yourself on track to act and feel worthy and deserving. Push yourself like never before to develop a worthy self and love yourself. I've always loved the biblical command "Love thy neighbor as thyself," because it demands that one love oneself as well as others. We are at our best and can truly love others only if we love ourselves. Worthiness is just that important.

The Best Part of Divorce

Divorce doesn't have only a negative effect on all children. Struggle does often develop some positive traits. My research found that 57 percent of adults who were children of divorce believe that the divorce made them more independent, 44 percent said it made them a better friend, and 38 percent said it made them very committed to their spouses. Although it may have taken some sad challenges of youth to develop these traits, you are still the beneficiary of turning those tough times into something good in your life.

That's the message of this book and of life itself. You can't control the curve balls that are thrown at you, but you can surely work to determine the effect they'll have on your life. You can change anything you want, and don't let your childhood of divorce tell you any different.

Persistence Pays

The primary difference between humans and the rest of the animal world is our ability to change and adapt. The very desire and effort to change who we are represents the very best of our human condition. But it is the hardest thing to do. It goes against our animal instincts, and it takes a courageous person to want to change. You have become that person. I understand that you may not be at the goal line yet. The truth is that no one ever is. But as long as you keep moving the ball forward, you are taking your life back and living it as you want.

It's now time to stop the negative buzzing in your brain and keep your compass pointed on your true north. With your new understanding of your truth and its effect on you, you will change and can never go back. Even if there are days when you think you haven't changed, believe me, you *have* changed. Just slow down the negative chatter going on internally, and you will feel it.

There may be times when you don't feel the change. Keep working at it. Sometimes you have to keep repeating things until you get them, then all of a sudden, *like wow*, you are different. It's like weight loss: a pound here and there isn't noticeable until you've lost a significant amount, and then you wake up and look in the mirror and notice a smaller you. One night at bedtime you'll look back on your day and realize you didn't act and think in the negative ways of your past. Then it'll turn into a week and eventually a month, and your new autopilot will finally be your own.

In my opinion, this effort to change is godly, and that is why my life is about people and connecting to them. Throughout this book, I have spoken to you as I would to any relative or friend I deeply want to help. In today's world of social media, there is no reason for our relationship to stop here. Visit me at my website, http://www.mgaryneuman.com, and on Facebook and Twitter at mgaryneuman.

Thank you for giving me the honor of helping you. *You are worth it!*

Index